SCRAPS, INC.

VOL.1

15 BLOCK-BASED DESIGNS FOR THE MODERN QUILTER

Compiled by
Susanne Woods

Published in 2014 by Lucky Spool Media, LLC

Lucky Spool Media, LLC
1005 Blackwood Lane, Lafayette, CA 94549
www.luckyspool.com
info@luckyspool.com

TEXT © Individual Designers
EDITOR Susanne Woods
ILLUSTRATIONS Kari Vojtechovsky
PHOTOGRAPHY © Lucky Spool Media, LLC
FRONT COVER DESIGNER Liz Quan
DESIGNER Kari Vojtechovsky

Note to copy shops: Pages 124–127 can be photocopied for personal use.

Photograph on page 13 of Alex Ledgerwood, page 60, and page 88 © Lauren Hunt
Photograph on page 51 of April Rosenthal © VIS-A-VIS Studio
Photograph on page 71 of Camille Roskelley © Marissa Girard Photography
Photograph on page 83 of Jeni Baker © Michael Hanna
Photograph on page 101 of Melissa Lunden © Peter Ellenby
Photograph on page 117 of Susan Beal © Nancy Flynn

9 8 7 6 5 4 3 2 1

First Edition
Printed and bound in the USA

Library of Congress Cataloging-in-Publication Data available upon request

ISBN: 978-1-940655-04-8
LSID 0014

CONTENTS

PROJECTS

Welcome to

SCRAPS, INC.

If you picked up this book, you are probably already a prolific quilt maker, with a love for every inch of the leftover fabrics from each quilt you've ever made. This has likely turned you into one of us: a scrap junkie.

We know who we are. We are the ones who look secretly and fondly through our scrap bins way more often than we should. We are the ones who buy, swap, and trade scraps among our fellow obsessives. So, if you are one of us, this is the book for you.

Scraps, Inc. features fifteen of the best designers in quilt making today and the scrappy patterns they created just for this book. We know that scrappy quilts are often the ones you keep for yourself, so we wanted to offer a series of designs that would fit well in any home…quilts that use the colors we are loving right now, combined with innovative, on-trend designs that are easy to live with.

Because each quilt pattern is block-based, quilt assembly is simple — which is welcome after working with all those little pieces from our scrap bins. We'll also tell you if the pattern is constructed using strips of fabric, squares of fabric, or both, to help you find the best project for your own unique scrap stash.

Each designer offers up her own tips for storing scraps, too, with the aim of keeping you both organized and inspired. Most of all, we hope that you rummage through your scrap bins, rediscover why you loved each piece of fabric, and use them all in one or many of these stunning quilts.

BASIC BLOCKS

Here are some basic block techniques that you will find helpful in the projects. Since this is a book about using fabric scraps, we think that you already know the basics of quilt making and have discovered certain techniques and methods of construction that have become favorites; however, if this is your first quilt making book or even if you just need a reminder of some of the basics, please download the free PDF available at luckyspool.com containing our Quilt Making Basics.

HALF-SQUARE TRIANGLE (AKA HST)

This is a simple way to make HSTs. This example creates a 2½'' unfinished block.

Figure 1. *Figure 2.* *Figure 3.*

1 Cut a 3'' square of fabric A and a 3'' square of a coordinating or contrasting fabric B (depending on the look you are going for). Cut squares ½'' larger than your unfinished HST unit.

2 Draw a diagonal line on the wrong side of each of the fabric A squares. (Figure 1)

3 Pair a fabric A square with a fabric B square, right sides together. Sew ¼'' away from both sides of the marked diagonal line using a ¼'' foot on your machine.

4 Cut along the drawn diagonal line, fold open along the seam line. (Figure 2)

5 Set the seams with a hot iron and press toward the darker fabric. Trim to 2½'' as needed. (Figure 3)

STRIP SETS

Many of the projects in this book use strip sets. Here are general instructions for creating these.

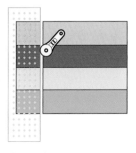

Figure 4.

1 Determine the unfinished dimensions (width and height) of the block needed as well as the number of strips in the block from the individual pattern instructions.

2 Arrange your cut strips by the colors indicated in the individual pattern. (Figure 4)

3 Stitch together each strip along the long side using a ¼'' seam allowance. Press the seams open or in a consistent direction for all of the strips in the block.

4 Once you have attached all of the strips, press and trim to the finished size or begin sub-cutting your strip set into separate units (Figure 4) as indicated in the individual pattern instructions.

QUILTER TO QUILTER
- -
To prevent your strips from distorting, alternate the direction you begin sewing each strip to your set. For example, if you attached the first strip sewing from the left side of the block to the right, attach your next strip beginning from the right side of the block, stitching toward to the left side.

THE PROJECTS

STRIPES EARNED

By Alex Ledgerwood

Quilted by
Tia Curtis

Use your gray, white, and chartreuse scraps to make this masculine quilt. The stone solid sets a neutral background for the chevrons, which are reminiscent of the three stripes of military insignia. The blocks are made from simple strip sets (see page 9), perfect for using up those leftover strips of fabrics from your favorite past projects. Don't worry about a special angled ruler or cutting from templates. Sew the straight strips together and I'll show you how to create the 60-degree angle later.

Love the quilt but have a rainbow of scraps? Create a completely different feel by using a light background and candy-colored scraps. Each stripe can be a different fabric, or group like colored scraps to create monochromatic chevrons.

Finished Block Size: 12″×13½″

Finished Quilt Size: 72″×93″

MATERIALS

Scraps (in gray, white, and chartreuse): (30) 2¼''×10'' strips of each color

Background Fabric: 6½ yards

Binding Fabric: ¾ yard

Backing Fabric: 5½ yards

Batting: 78''×99''

Special Tools: 6''×24'' acrylic ruler with 60-degree angle marking

CUTTING

Note: Width of Fabric = WOF

From Each Scrap Color Group, cut:
- (30) strips 2¼''×10''

From Background Fabric, cut:
- (2) 6½''×72½'' strips
- (2) 6½''×81½'' strips
- (15) 12½''×14'' rectangles
- (60) 4''×10'' strips
- (60) 2¼''×10'' strips

From Binding Fabric, cut:
- (9) strips 2½''× WOF

QUILTER TO QUILTER

When triming blocks with bias edges, it is helpful to use spray starch both prior to cutting and each time you press a seam. The extra stiffness will help prevent distortion. Be careful to handle the blocks as little as possible and press carefully to avoid stretching.

ASSEMBLING THE BLOCKS

To make each block you will need:

- (2) 2¼''×10''scraps strips of each of the three colors
- (4) 4''×10''strips of background fabric
- (4) 2¼''×10'' strips of background fabric

Piecing the Strip Sets

1 To help picture the finished block, lay out the strips in order with the strips for each half of the block angling in opposite directions (Figure 1). Both halves of the block will begin with a 4''×10'' background piece. Alternate scrap strips separated by background fabric of the same size, ending in another 4''×10'' rectangle.

2 Piece the strips. Anticipate the angle at which they will eventually be trimmed by staggering the strips 1'' as you begin each seam. The sides of the block will be staggered in opposite directions (Figure 1).

3 Repeat to create 30 strip sets: 15 will angle to the left and 15 will angle to the right.

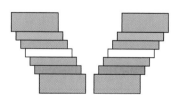

Figure 1.

Trimming the Blocks

1 Locate the 60-degree angle on your ruler. Align with the top seam on the left half of the block, placing the ruler as close to the right edge of the strip set as possible without going past the edge of any of the strips. Trim away any excess fabric to the right of the ruler. (Figure 2)

2 Turn the block so that the cut side is aligned with a vertical line on your cutting mat. Measure 6½" from the cut edge and trim away the excess.

3 Trim the two remaining edges perpendicular to the other edges to create a 6½"×14" rectangle. (Figure 3)

4 Repeat for the remaining left halves of the blocks.

5 To trim the 15 right halves of the blocks, flip the ruler over (so the underside of the ruler faces up) to cut the opposite angle. With the ruler underside up, it will create the complementary 60-degree angle from those cut in Step 1.

6 Repeat the above instructions for the remaining right halves of the blocks.

7 Carefully aligning and pinning your seams as you go, sew a left half and a right half of a block together. (Figure 4)

8 Repeat to complete the remaining 14 block units.

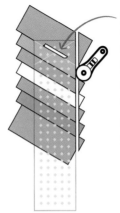

Figure 2.

QUILTER TO QUILTER

Add a strip of masking, painters, or washi tape along the 60° line on your ruler to make it easier to see from the underside as you trim.

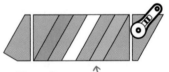

Figure 3.

QUILTER TO QUILTER

You may wish to initially cut this unit to 14½", then trim to 14" after piecing the two sides together. This will allow you to trim an exact ¼" from the chevron point.

Figure 4.

ASSEMBLING THE QUILT TOP

1 To create the top row (Row A), sew together three striped blocks with two 12½''×14'' background rectangles (Figure 5), beginning and ending with a striped block. Be sure the chevron points on all striped blocks are on the bottom edge of the block, pointing down.

2 Make a total of three Row A's.

3 To create Row B, sew together three 12½''×14'' background rectangles with two striped blocks, beginning and ending with background rectangles.

4 Make a total of three Row B's.

5 Sew the rows together, alternating Row A and Row B, beginning with Row A at the top.

6 Attach 6½''×81½'' borders to the left and right edge of the unit.

7 Attach 6½''×72½'' borders to the top and bottom of the unit.

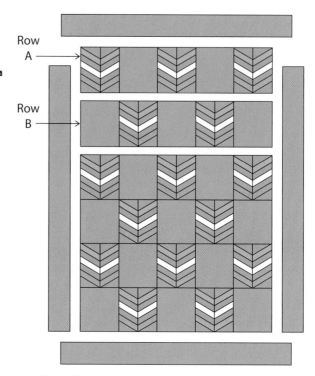

Row A →

Row B →

Figure 5.

FINISHING THE QUILT

Layer the quilt top, batting, and backing fabric. Baste, quilt, and bind using your favorite method.

SCRAP STASH TIPS From Alex Ledgerwood

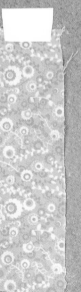

I generally like to cut scraps into usable sizes as I'm working on other projects. Any time I cut fabric for a project and have less than a quarter yard leftover, I cut the remaining fabric into strips and squares.

I store scraps together by size. I have a bin for 2½" strips, another bin for strips that are less than 2½" wide, a bin of 2½" squares, and finally a basket for teeny scraps less than 2½" square. (Yes, I may have a problem.) This system means I have scraps ready to use for a variety of projects whenever the mood strikes.

For leftover fabric that is closer to fat quarter size, I keep the scrap intact and store it by color in plastic shoe boxes. These scraps can be used for small projects like zippy bags or scrappy quilting projects. Storing the fabrics by color means I can easily find just what I need, just when I need it.

BANGLES

By Allison Harris

Quilted by Christina Lane

I've always been drawn to chain quilts. They are timeless, simple, and a great way to use scraps. I added a simple four-patch block and appliqué diamonds to create this version. The diamond blocks remind me of jewels, so I chose modern shades of purple, coral, teal, green, and yellow. Try using a darker background fabric with light fabrics for the chain squares to make a different, but equally beautiful look.

Finished Block Size: 6″ square
Finished Quilt Size: 54″×72″

MATERIALS

Scraps, Print and Solid Colors:
- (44) 2"×21" strips,
  or (22) 2"× WOF strips cut
  from yardage and cut in half
- 54 squares at least 2¾"

Background Fabric: 3 yards

Binding Fabric: ½ yard

Backing Fabric: 3¾ yards

Batting: 60"×78"

Fusible Web: approximately 1 yard
lightweight double-sided fusible web

CUTTING

Note: Width of Fabric = WOF

From Background Fabric, cut:
- (9) 2"×WOF strips;
  subcut into (12) 2"×3½" strips,
  108 total
- (6) 3½"×WOF strips;
  subcut into (2) 3½"×21" strips,
  11 total
- (9) 6½"×WOF strips;
  subcut each into (6) 6½" squares,
  54 total

From Binding Fabric, cut:
- (7) 2½"×WOF strips

Chain Block

Diamond Block

QUILTER TO QUILTER

Using a neutral fabric with a slight
texture adds depth to the quilt.
The cream fabric I used is Quilters
Linen in Snow by Robert Kaufman.

ASSEMBLING THE BLOCKS

Chain Blocks

1 From the 22 scrap strips, sew the strips into pairs right sides together, press seams to one side. You will have 11 strip sets (see page 9).

2 Subcut each strip set into (10) 2″ wide units, 108 total.

3 Lay out two of the strip set units long sides together and rotate them as needed so the seams face opposite directions, creating locking seams. (Figure 1)

4 Pin and sew the units together. Press seams to one side. Repeat until you have made 54 four-patch blocks.

5 Pin and sew a background 2″×3½″ strip to both sides of each four-patch block to create Row 2 (Figure 2). Press seams in toward the four-patch. Repeat for the remaining 53 four-patch blocks.

6 Choose two of the remaining 2″×21″ scrap strips and attach to either side of a background 3½″×21″ strip. Sew the strips right sides together and press seams out toward the scrap strips. Repeat until you've made 11 strip sets.

7 Place the strip sets on the cutting mat, and cut each strip set into (10) 2″ wide units, 108 total.

8 Pin and sew a strip set unit to the top and bottom of each four-patch block (Figure 2). Press seams away from the center. The block should measure 6½″ square. Repeat to create 54 chain blocks.

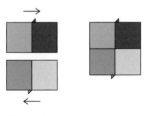

Figure 1.

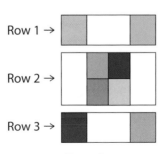

Row 1 →
Row 2 →
Row 3 →

Figure 2.

QUILTER TO QUILTER

These blocks go together quickly with chain piecing. To do this, sew the pieces together one after another without stopping to clip threads until the very end and this top will go together in no time!

Diamond Blocks

1 Fuse each of the 54 scrap squares to the fusible web, following the product instructions. Cut each fused piece into a 2½'' square.

2 Choose a scrap square and peel the paper off the back to expose the fusible web. Fold a background 6½'' square in half each way, finger pressing to create crease marks. Refer to shaded lines in Figure 3.

3 On the ironing board, align the corners of a 2½'' scrap square along the crease marks so the scrap square is centered in the background square. Iron the square to fuse it in place.

4 Use a small zigzag stitch or blanket stitch to stitch around the edges of the scrap square and secure it in place.

5 Repeat Steps 2 through 4 with the remaining scrap and background squares until you've made a total of 54 diamond blocks.

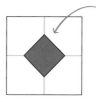

Figure 3.

QUILTER TO QUILTER

I used invisible thread to secure my squares to the background. Invisible thread can be found at most quilt shops and works perfectly for sewing around the diamond edges for a nearly invisible finish.

SCRAP STASH TIPS From Allison Harris

Since I go from project to project quickly, my scrap bins easily get full and out of control. Because of that, I've made a habit of organizing my scraps as soon as I'm done cutting out the project I'm working on. First I press my scraps so they take up less space in my bins. Then I sort them into two bins, one for squares or larger pieces, and one for strips. If my pieces and strips are odd sizes, I quickly trim them down so the piece is usable. It takes only a minute and it allows me to find scraps easily and fit more in the bin!

Project 2: Bangles

Figure 4.

ASSEMBLING THE QUILT TOP

1 Referring to Figure 4, lay out the blocks into 12 rows of nine blocks each, starting with a chain block in the top left corner and alternating blocks as shown.

2 Pin and sew the blocks together to form the rows. Press seams toward the diamond blocks.

3 Pin and sew the rows together. Press.

FINISHING THE QUILT

Layer the quilt top, batting, and backing fabric. Baste, quilt, and bind using your favorite method.

MY FAVORITE THINGS

By Amy Ellis

Some of my most-loved quilts are scrap quilts. The fabric combinations are happy and often mismatched, which adds a bit of whimsy.

For this project, I decided to focus on some of my favorite traditional blocks, and incorporate them into a scrappy medallion quilt. To ensure that my quilt would be the perfect size for snuggling, I started with a rectangle of blocks in the center and worked out from there. I love the myriad neutrals mixed with all the orange, yellow, green, and purple fabrics from my scrap bin. This quilt will be a fixture in my house for a long time to come. Feel free to swap out your favorite 3″ or 6″ blocks to make this medallion quilt uniquely yours!

Finished Block Sizes: 3″ and 6″ squares
Finished Quilt Size: 60″×78″

MATERIALS

Scraps: approximately 1½ yards of each orange, green, yellow, and purple fabric scraps

Background Fabric: approximately 5¼ yards total of assorted neutral fabrics, in cream and gray tones

Border Fabric: 1 yard

Binding Fabric: ⅝ yard

Backing Fabric: 4 yards

Batting: 66″×84″

QUILTER TO QUILTER

A perfect ¼″ seam allowance is helpful in general quilt making but crucial in a medallion setting. Test your ¼″ seam allowance by sewing two 2½″ squares together, and check your results. If your sewn piece doesn't measure 4½″ across, adjust your seam allowance and recheck the results.

CUTTING

Note: Width of Fabric = WOF

Star Blocks

From Scraps, cut:
- (10) 3½″ squares
- (40) 2⅜″ squares

From Background Fabrics, cut:
- (40) 2″ squares
- (10) 4¼″ squares

Four-Patch Blocks

From Scraps, cut:
- (1) 2″×WOF strip, for strip piecing four-patch blocks (I used yellow)

From Background Fabrics, cut:
- (9) 2″×WOF strips from a variety of different fabrics, for strip piecing four-patch blocks

Triangles

From Scraps, cut:
- (11) 4″×20″ strips

From Background Fabrics, cut:
- (5) 4″×WOF strips
- (4) 3½″ squares

Churn Dash Blocks

From 42 Scrap Frabics, cut:
- (2) 3" squares and (1) 1½"×12" strip for each of the 42 churn dash blocks
- (1) 2½" square for 21 churn dash blocks

From 42 Background Fabrics, cut:
- (2) 3" squares and (1) 1½"×12" strip for each of 42 churn dash blocks
- (1) 2½" square for 21 churn dash blocks

Log Cabin Blocks

From Scraps, cut:
- (20) 3½"×WOF strips
- (10) 2½"×WOF strips; subcut into 1½" rectangles as needed, for paper piecing log cabin blocks

From Background Fabrics, cut:
- (52) 1½" light center squares
- (52) 1½" dark center squares
- (20) 3½"×WOF strips
- (10) 2½"×WOF strips; subcut into 1½" rectangles as needed, for paper piecing log cabin blocks

Note: These log cabin numbers are approximate, as you might not have full width of fabric to cut from for most scraps, or you may be able to use a leftover scrap already sewn into the block earlier and trimmed away. I recommend that you cut as you sew for this block, and keep the scrap bin nearby to dip into as needed.

Plain Borders

From Background Fabrics, cut:
(17) 2"×WOF strips for borders; subcut into:
- (2) 2"×15½" rectangles
- (2) 2"×30½" rectangles
- (2) 2"×24½" rectangles
- (2) 2"×39½" rectangles
- (2) 2"×36½" rectangles
- (2) 2"×54½" rectangles
- (2) 2"×45½" pieced rectangles
- (2) 2"×63½" pieced rectangles
- (8) 2" squares

From Binding Fabric, cut:

- (8) strips, 2½"×WOF

ASSEMBLING THE BLOCKS

Star Blocks

1 Mark a diagonal line on the wrong side of four 2⅜″ squares. (Figure 1)

2 Pair two of the marked squares with the neutral 4¼″ square, slightly overlapping in the center (Figure 2). Sew ¼″ away from both sides of the marked diagonal lines.

3 Cut the sewn units between the seam lines (Figure 3). Press the seam allowances away from the neutral square. (Figure 4)

4 Add the remaining marked square to the unit. Sew ¼″ away from both sides of the marked diagonal line (Figure 5). Cut apart the flying geese on the marked diagonal (Figure 6). Press the seam allowances away from the neutral triangle. Trim to 2″×3½″ if necessary (Figure 7). Repeat for the remaining units to create four flying geese units.

5 Lay out the Star Block with the 3½″ square in the middle and the 2″ sqaures at each corner (Figure 8). Sew the pieces into rows and press the seam allowances in opposite directions. Sew the rows together, pressing the seam allowances in opposite directions.

6 Repeat Steps 1–5 to create 10 Star Blocks.

QUILTER TO QUILTER

I suggest piecing the larger blocks before starting on the smaller Log Cabin Blocks. This will allow you to collect even more scraps for all the pieces that go into each of those blocks.

Figure 1.   *Figure 2.*

Figure 3.   *Figure 4.*

Figure 5.   *Figure 6.*   *Figure 7.*

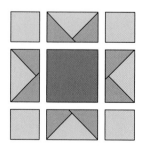

Figure 8.

Four-Patch Blocks

1 Sew the (10) 2″ strips into pairs right side together (see page 9). Four of your strip sets will be neutrals only. One will have the scrap strip that you chose along with a background (I used yellow).

2 Press the seam allowances to one side. Subcut (96) 2″ units.

3 Match the units, being sure to vary where the scrap fabric squares are pieced (Figure 9), nest the seams, and sew 48 Four-Patch blocks. Press the seam allowances in one direction. (Figure 10)

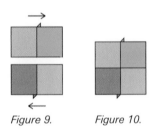

Figure 9.   *Figure 10.*

QUILTER TO QUILTER

Trim your HST units before you press them open so there are only two sides to trim! Use the corner of a small square ruler to line up the seam at the 2½″ marks and trim away. Also, make sure you are using a fine thread (40wt–50wt) that doesn't eat up a lot of space in your seam allowance.

Triangles

1 From background fabric strips, cut 48 from Template A (see page 124) and 8 from Template B (see page 124).

2 From scrap strips, cut 52 from Template A and set aside.

Churn Dash Blocks

1 Separate your cut units so that you have one background fabric set, and one scrap fabric set for each of the 42 blocks. Half will have a colorful background, half will have a neutral background.

2 Create four HST units from the 3″ squares (see page 9).

3 Sew the 1½″×12″ rectangles together, side by side. Press to the darker fabric, and cut four segments 2½″ each.

4 Lay out the block as shown in Figure 11 with a corresponding 2½″ square in the center. Sew the rows together. Press the seam allowances in alternate directions for each row.

5 Pin and sew the block rows together. Press rows outward.

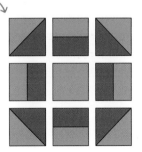

Figure 11.

Log Cabin Blocks

1 Make 104 copies of the Log Cabin paper pattern (page 124). Up to four patterns will fit on one page.

2 Start in the center with a light or dark square. Add a small strip, making sure to cover the seam line with at least ¼", and sew on the line (Figure 12). I alternated my light and dark centers, and ended with the opposite value to differentiate each block in the quilt top.

3 Fold back the paper to the sewn seam and trim to a ¼" seam allowance using a rotary cutter and ruler.

4 Press the fabric over the seam allowance. Continue working in the same manner until all the pieces have been added.

5 After pressing the last piece in place, trim the excess to the dotted outside seam allowance line on all four sides.

6 Keep the papers in place until the entire top is finished.

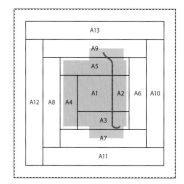

Figure 12.

Paper Piecing

If you haven't paper pieced before, here are a few tips to get you started.

- Shorten your stitch length to 1.5mm. This makes less work of removing the papers later.

- The printed side of the pattern is the reverse of the finished block; make sure that the right side of the fabric is up before pressing the seam allowance.

- Hold the paper and the fabric piece up to the light to verify that you have enough seam allowance before stitching.

- Make an extra copy of the block if you want to practice.

- Sew all of one block, or chain piece like you might other blocks.

- I like to set up my sewing space with all the tools I will need. I keep the iron and cutting mat close by so that I can quickly move on to the next step!

- Refer to Amy Friend's project on page 40 for step-by-step instructions on how to paper piece blocks.

Tip: My favorite ruler for paper piecing is the Add-A-Quarter ruler by CM Designs, Inc.

ASSEMBLING THE QUILT TOP

Star Block

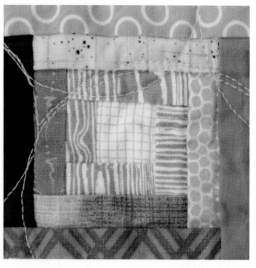

Log Cabin Block

1 Using Figure 13 (see page 32) as a reference, lay out two columns of five Star Blocks for the center, nesting the seam allowances.

2 Sew five pairs together and press the seam allowances in opposite directions. Sew the five rows together. Press the seam allowances in one direction.

3 Attach the first border. Sew the side strips using the 2″×30½″ background strips. Press the seam allowances toward the border. Attach the top and bottom strips using the 2″×15½″ background strips. Press the seam allowances toward the border again.

4 Sew 2 sets of 11 Log Cabin Blocks, starting with a dark center and alternating with a light center. Press the seam allowances in one direction. Pin and sew these sets to the sides of the medallion, easing fabric as needed. Press the seam allowance toward the border.

5 Sew two sets of seven Log Cabin Blocks in a row, starting with a light center and alternating with a dark center. Press the seam allowances so that they will nest with the attached blocks from Step 4. Pin and sew these sets to the top and bottom of the medallion, easing fabric as needed. Press the seam allowances toward the border.

Figure 13.

Project 3: My Favorite Things

Colorful Triangle Strips

6 Attach the second border. Sew the side strips using the 2″×39½″strips. Press the seam allowances toward the border. Attach the top and bottom borders using the 2″×24½″ strips. Press the seam allowances toward the border again.

7 Sew two sets of 14 Four-Patch blocks in a row, pressing the seam allowances in one direction. Pin and sew these sets to the sides of the medallion, easing fabric as needed. Press the seam allowances toward the border.

8 Sew two sets of 10 Four-Patch blocks in a row. Press the seam allowances so that they nest with the blocks from Step 7. Sew these sets to the top and bottom of the medallion, easing fabric as needed. Press the seam allowances toward the border.

9 Sew two sets of 16 colorful Triangles together in a row, alternating the scraps and the 15 background Triangles. Attach a Template B to both ends of the rows. Press all the seam allowances toward the colorful Triangles. Pin and sew these sets to the sides of the medallion, easing fabric as needed. Press the seam allowances toward the four-patch blocks.

10 Sew two sets of 10 colorful Triangles in a row with 9 background Triangles and two end pieces. Press all the seam allowances toward the colorful Triangles. Add (4) 3½″ squares to both ends of these sets. Pin and sew to the top and bottom of the medallion, easing fabric as needed. Press the seam allowances toward the four-patch blocks.

11 Add the third round of borders. Sew the side strips using the 2″×54½″ strips, pressing the seam allowances toward the border. (I suggest sewing with the triangle border on top so you are less likely to loose those beautiful points.) Sew a 2″ background square to each end of the 2″×36½″ borders, then pin and sew to the top and bottom of the medallion, easing fabric as needed. Press the seam allowances toward the border.

12 Sew two sets of 19 Log Cabin blocks in a row, starting with a light center and alternating with a dark center. Press the seam allowances in one direction. Pin and sew these sets to the sides of the medallion, easing fabric as needed. Press the seam allowances toward the border.

Churn Dash Block

13 Sew two sets of 15 Log Cabin Blocks in a row, starting with a dark center and alternating with a light center. Press the seam allowances so that they will nest with the blocks attached in Step 12. Pin and sew sets to the top and bottom of the medallion, easing fabric as needed. Press the seam allowances toward the border.

14 Add the fourth round of borders. Sew the side strips using the 2″×63½″ strips. Press the seam allowances toward the border. Sew a 2″ background square to each end of the 2″×45½″ borders, then pin and sew to the top and bottom of the medallion, easing fabric as needed. Press the seam allowances toward the border.

SCRAP STASH TIPS From Amy Ellis

In my studio, scraps are usually set aside as I cut, and again as I finish a project. I keep a large plastic tote under my long arm quilting machine, for stowing scraps quickly and easily. Then when I'm ready to start a scrappy project, I can pull them out and sort by color. I like to keep scraps within reach, but out of the way. Sewing from the scrap bin is always a treat, and usually serves as a reminder of the other quilts I've made in the recent past.

15 Sew two sets of 11 Churn Dash Blocks in a row, alternating backgrounds. Press the seam allowances in one direction. Pin and sew these sets to the sides of the medallion, easing fabric as needed. Press the seam allowances toward the border.

16 Sew two sets of 10 Churn Dash Blocks in a row, alternating backgrounds. Press the seam allowances so that they will nest with the attached blocks from Step 15. Pin and sew sets to the top and bottom of the medallion, easing fabric as needed. Press the seam allowances toward the border to complete the quilt top.

FINISHING THE QUILT

Remove the papers from the backs of each of the Log Cabin blocks. Layer the quilt top, batting, and backing fabric. Baste, quilt, and bind using your favorite method.

TWINKLE

By Amy Friend

Paper piecing is my favorite piecing technique. This particular design lends itself well to scraps. Each block is just 6″ square so even the smallest of scraps can be used. This quilt would look really striking in solids, but it was more fun to sew scrappy! The blocks create a crisscrossing design with a pattern of pinwheels at the junctions. The background creates a secondary diamond pattern.

I pulled a specific range of yellows, greens, and grays. The grays create the pinwheels. I divided my scraps into seven piles from lightest to darkest shades of mustard, green, and citron for piecing the wedges. I pulled from each pile for specific sections of the pattern template. This little bit of organization can help when you are dealing with scraps, or you could throw caution to the wind and just pull from whichever piles you like.

Finished Block Size: 6″ square
Finished Quilt Size: 60″×72″

MATERIALS

Scraps: a variety of scraps loosely arranged into seven color families and ranging in size from 2½''×3½'' to 3''×6''

Background Fabric: 3 yards

Binding Fabric: ½ yard

Backing Fabric: 4 yards

Batting: 66''×78''

QUILTER TO QUILTER

Many of these pieces can be cut from 2½''-wide precut strips and binding scraps as well as fabric squares, so be sure to search through your whole stash.

CUTTING

Note: Width of Fabric = WOF

Color Group 1 (A1), cut:
- (120) 3''×6'' rectangles

Color Group 2 (A2), cut:
- (120) 2½''×4'' rectangles

Color Group 3 (A3), cut:
- (120) 3''×5½'' rectangles

Color Group 4 (A4), cut:
- (120) 3''×5'' rectangles

Color Group 5 (A5), cut:
- (120) 2½''×4½'' rectangles

Color Group 6 (A6), cut:
- (120) 3½''×4'' rectangles

Color Group 7 (A7), cut:
- (120) 2½''×3½'' rectangles

From Binding Fabric, cut:
- (7) 2½''×WOF strips

From Background Fabric, cut:
- (120) 5''×7'' rectangles; subcut on the diagonal to create 240 right triangles

Size Options

These instructions are for creating a lap-size quilt. If you would like to make a different size, use the chart below to calculate how many blocks you will need.

	Lap	Twin	Queen
Finished Size	60''×72''	72''×84''	90''×96''
Number of Pieced Blocks	120	168	240
Pieced Blocks per Row	10	12	15
Number of Rows	12	14	16

SCRAP STASH TIPS From Amy Friend

When I am cleaning up after a project, I simply refold my fabric and include any scraps of that fabric inside the folds and put it back up on my shelf in color order. I do not reserve my shelf space for yardage only. When I first started quilting, I used a scrap bag but rarely took the time to sort through it. With my new system, I do use most of my scraps. If I have a really small piece of something left, I might run it through a fabric cutting machine using either the 2″ square or 2½″ half-square triangle die and throw them into a bag for a "someday" project.

ASSEMBLING THE BLOCKS

1 Print 120 copies of the pattern template (see page 125).

2 Place the fabric for A1 with the wrong side against the back of your template and the right side facing out. Make sure that the fabric extends about ¼'' past the stitching line between section A1 and A2. Place the fabric for section A2 on top of the fabric for A1, right sides together. Flip your paper and stitch along the line (Figure 1). Press.

3 Place the fabric for A3 on A1, right sides together and extending at least ¼'' over the stitching line. Flip your paper and stitch along the line between sections A1 and A3. Trim the seam allowance to ¼'' (Figure 2). Press.

4 Place the fabric for A4 on A3, right sides together and extending at least ¼'' over the stitching line. Flip paper and stitch along the line between section A3 and A4. Trim the seam allowance to ¼'' (Figure 3). Press.

5 Continue adding pieces to your paper template in numerical order. Use the background triangles for pieces 8 and 9. (Figures 4–7)

6 Trim block along the seam allowance line. Your unfinished block should measure 6½'' square. (Figure 8)

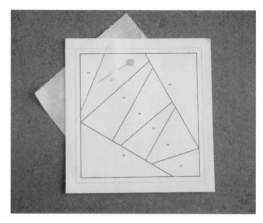

Figure 1.

Figure 2.

Figure 3.

Project 4: Twinkle

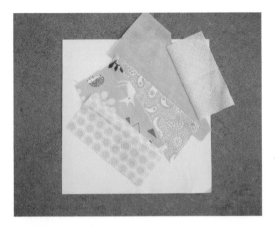

Figure 4.

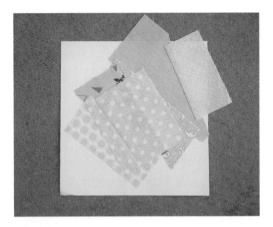

Figure 5.

Figure 6.

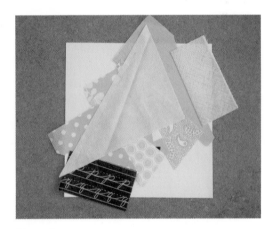

Figure 7.

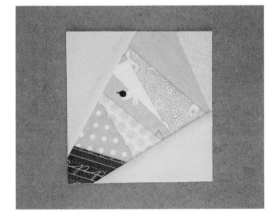

Figure 8.

QUILTER TO QUILTER
- -
Prepare for paper piecing by changing
your needle to a size 90/14 and reducing
your stitch length to about 1.6mm. Print
your templates on copy paper or paper
specifically made for paper piecing.

Figure 9.

ASSEMBLING THE QUILT TOP

1 Sew the blocks together in pairs, matching the A7 sections, to create 60 units (Figure. 9). Press all seams to the right.

2 Join the 60 pairs to create 30 big blocks, again matching the A7 sections. Nest your seams.

3 Arrange your blocks as desired, assembling them into six rows of five big blocks. Press seams alternating the direction for each row. Sew the rows together. (Figure 10)

FINISHING THE QUILT

Remove the paper from the back of each of the blocks. Layer the quilt top, batting, and backing fabric. Baste, quilt, and bind using your favorite method.

Figure 10.

SCRAPPY
COURTHOUSE STEPS

**By Amy
Smart**

*Quilted by
Melissa Kelley*

One of my favorite blocks for using up scraps of fabric is a traditional log cabin or its courthouse steps variation. It's nice and easy to hack up all those scraps into a variety of uniform sizes and put together a block quickly. I also love these blocks because they're fun to make "scrappy" — just picking up random prints in the next size strip you need. They always turn out great.

This project uses scraps that are only 1½" wide and a variety of lengths, making it easy to pull a good assortment of fabrics. For this project I picked two large contrasting color families. Given the size of my scrap storage, that meant I had a lot of scraps options with very few designs repeated.

Finished Block Size: 10" square

Finished Quilt Size: 60"×80"

MATERIALS

Scraps:
- an assortment of light-colored scraps (low-volume prints, creams, and grays)
- an assortment of warm-colored scraps (reds, oranges, golds)
- an assortment of cool-colored scraps (turquoises, blues, purples)

Center Square Fabric:
¼ yard of a dark gray solid

Binding Fabric: ½ yard

Backing Fabric: 5 yards

Batting: 66″×86″

CUTTING

Note: Width of Fabric = WOF

From Dark Gray Solid, cut:
- (3) 2½″×WOF strips; subcut into (48) 2½″ squares (Unit A)

From Light-Colored Scraps, cut:
- (96) 1½″×2½″ rectangles (Unit B)
- (96) 1½″×4½″ rectangles (Unit C)
- (96) 1½″×6½″ rectangles (Unit D)
- (96) 1½″×8½″ rectangles (Unit E)

From Warm and Cool Scraps, cut:
- (48) 1½″×4½″ strips each of warm and cool (Unit C)
- (48) 1½″×6½″ rectangles each of warm and cool (Unit D)
- (48) 1½″×8½″ rectangles each of warm and cool (Unit E)
- (48) 1½″×10½″ rectablges each of warm and cool (Unit F)

From Binding Fabric, cut:
- (7) 2½″×WOF strips

ASSEMBLING THE BLOCKS

1 Sew light-colored 1½″×2½″ strips (B) to opposite sides of a gray 2½″ square (A). Press seams away from the center. (Figure 1)

2 Sew a warm 1½″×4½″ strip (C) to one side of the block and a cool 1½″×4½″ strip (C) to the other side. Press seams away from the center. (Figure 2)

Figure 1.

Figure 2.

QUILTER TO QUILTER

Before you press your new strips open, "set the seam" by pressing on the closed seam. Then open up the new strips and press from the front to make sure the seam is open and those new pieces lay nice and flat.

3 Sew light-colored 1½"×4½" strips (C) to opposite sides of the block and press seams away from the center. (Figure 3)

Figure 3.

4 Sew a warm 1½"×6½" strip (D) to the warm side of the block, and a cool 1½"×6½" strip (D) to the cool side. Press seams away from the center.

5 Sew light-colored 1½"×6½" strips (D) to opposite sides of the block and press seams away from the center.

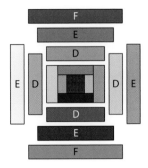

6 Sew a warm 1½"×8½" strip (E) to the warm side of the block and a cool 1½"×8½" strip (E) to the cool side. Press seams away from the center.

Figure 4.

7 Sew light-colored 1½"×8½" strips (E) to opposite sides of the block and press seams away from the center.

8 Sew a warm 1½"×10½" strip (F) to the warm side of the block. Press seam away from the center. Sew a cool 1½"×10½" strip (F) to the cool side. *Only on this one seam*, press toward the center of the block. This will help with assembling the quilt blocks later. (Figure 4)

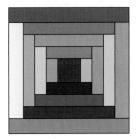

Figure 5.

9 Make a total of 48 blocks. (Figure 5)

ASSEMBLING THE QUILT TOP

1 Referring to Figure 6, lay out a row of six quilt blocks, alternating the directions the warm and cool sides are facing.

2 Lay out the second row of six blocks, matching the warm ends and cool ends with the colorways from the previous row.

3 Repeat this layout for a total of eight rows of six blocks each. Make sure you get a balance of colors and prints spread throughout the quilt.

4 Sew blocks into eight rows. Press seams in one row all in one direction, alternating directions on alternating rows (i.e., all seams to the left on odd rows and to the right on even rows).

5 Sew rows together, pressing seams in one direction.

FINISHING THE QUILT

Layer the quilt top, batting, and backing fabric. Baste, quilt, and bind using your favorite method.

SCRAP STASH TIPS From Amy Smart

I don't deny it: I am a scrap lover/hoarder. I have a hard time letting go of any of those little fabric orphans because I see the potential in each one. That said, one of the most important things I have learned regarding scraps is to keep only the ones that inspire you to actually do something with them. It's important to go through your scraps regularly and purge — just get rid of the ones you don't love anymore. This doesn't mean you have to throw them away — bundle them up and give them to a friend, or a guild, or someone else who would love to have them. Out-of-control scraps are not inspiring.

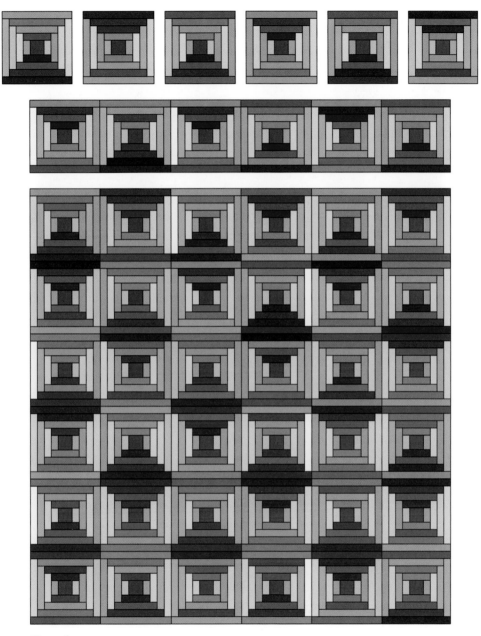

Figure 6.

OVERCAST

By April Rosenthal

To me, this quilt looks like like umbrellas on a street, from above. Gray skies, people taking cover, and streetlights reflecting on the pavement.

I started it with a traditional Irish chain block. As I progresed, I started seeing a secondary pattern that could be amazing with just the right fabrics and incorporating a simple curved line. The secondary design created by that white curved piecing really steals the show.

This is a perfect starter project for sewists new to curved piecing. Nearly all the blocks can be chain pieced, and most shapes are compatible with widely available cutting machine dies.

Be sure to choose a grounding "background" for your quilt. A strong solid here will help the rest of your piecing stand out, and provide much-needed contrast to the fabrics with a white background and to the scrappy colored strips.

Finished Block Size: 7½'' square

Finished Quilt Size: 62½'' square

MATERIALS

Scraps:
- approximately 1½ yards total of scraps in red, orange, yellow, green, aqua, and navy
- approximately ⅜ yard total of black scraps
- approximately 1½ yards total of scraps with white/light background

Background Fabric: 3 yards

Binding Fabric: ½ yard

Backing Fabric: 4 yards

Batting: 69″×69″

Fabric Glue Stick

QUILTER TO QUILTER

Shot cottons are beautiful fabrics that are made using two different colored threads woven in opposite directions to create a final look that is a mixture of both colors. They are usually a looser weave than regular quilting cotton, so be careful not to handle or distress cut edges more than necessary — they will fray easily. I used shot cotton as my background fabric in this project.

CUTTING

Note: Width of Fabric = WOF

From Gray Background Fabric, cut:
- 25 from Full-Curve Template (page 126)
- 12 from Half-Curve Template (page 126)
- 4 from Quarter-Curve Template (page 126)
- (496) 2″ squares
- (7) 2″×40″ strips (border)

From White/Light Fabrics, cut:
- 128 from Pie Piece template (see page 126)
- (256) 2″ squares

From Black Scraps, cut:
- (128) 2″ squares

From Red, Orange, Yellow, Green, Aqua, and Navy Scraps, cut:
24 of the following FULL SETS (each set the same color):
- (2) 2″ squares
- (2) 5″×2″ strips
- (1) 8″×2″ strip

16 of the following HALF SETS (each set the same color):
- (1) 2″ square
- (1) 5″×2″ strip

From Binding Fabric, cut:
- (7) 2½″×WOF strips

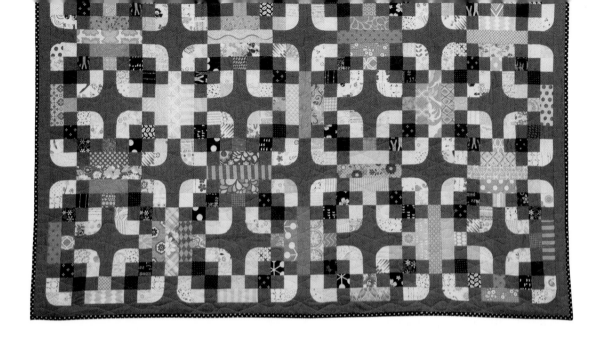

ASSEMBLING SQUARE UNITS

You will need the following square units to make this quilt:

BG Unit
Make 128.

GWGWG Unit
Make 62.

WGW Unit
Make 50.

WG Unit
Make 4.

1 Using cut 2″ squares, chain piece the following units:

- 128 black + gray background units (This uses all of your black squares.) (BG Unit)

- 62 gray + white/light + gray + white/light + gray units (GWGWG Unit)

- 50 white/light + gray + white/light units (WGW Unit)

- 4 white/light + gray units (WG Unit)

2 Press all seams toward the gray background fabric.

QUILTER TO QUILTER

With hundreds of small squares, chain piecing is a must for this quilt. In fact, when I chain pieced these units, I didn't clip anything apart until all the units were completely pieced. For speed, keep units connected and simply restart at the top of the chain when you're ready to add the next piece.

ASSEMBLING CURVE UNITS

You will need the following
curve units to make this quilt:

Quarter-Curve Unit
Assemble with one Quarter-Curve
Template and one Pie Piece Template.
Make 4.

Half-Curve Unit
Assemble with one Half-Curve Template
and two Pie Piece Templates. Make 12.

Full-Curve Unit
Assemble with one Full-Curve Template
and four Pie Piece Templates. Make 25.

1 Select one gray background quarter-curve piece and one pie piece to glue baste.

2 On the right side of the pie piece, place a thin line of glue on half of the curved edge.

3 With right sides together, match the approximate center of the pie piece and quarter-curve piece (Figure 1). Working gradually, match and press quarter-curve piece to pie piece along glued edge. (Figure 2)

4 Lifting quarter-curve piece out of the way, place a thin line of glue on the second half of the curved edge on the pie piece. (Figure 3)

5 Working gradually, match and press remaining half of quarter-curve piece to pie piece until the entire curved edge of the background fabric is secured with the glue. (Figure 4)

6 Repeat Steps 1–5 to glue baste remaining curve units for a total of four for the quarter-curve, 12 half-curve, and 25 full-curve units, always basting the gray background fabric onto the top of the pie pieces.

The full-curve, half-curve, quarter-curve and pie piece templates are on page 126.

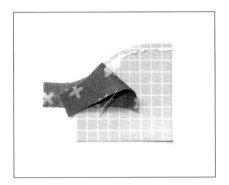

Figure 1.

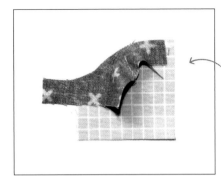

Figure 2.

Pie Piece template is intentionally large to allow flexibility in piecing. You will trim overage after pressing.

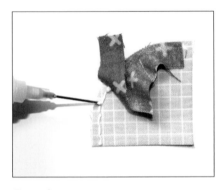

Figure 3.

Figure 4.

7 For all glue basted curve units, sew ¼" along the glued edge with the curved pie piece facing up. By stitching the blocks in this way, you will be able to prevent puckers and gathers. Chain piece all curved edges. Press seams toward pie piece.

8 Trim the the four quarter-curve units to 2" square, the 12 half-curve units to 2"×5", and the 25 full-curve units to 5" square. Set aside.

QUILTER TO QUILTER

There are many ways to baste and piece curves. I used the glue basting method because it doesn't require any special tools and is great for beginners to curved piecing. As you gain confidence, you may find that a specialty presser foot or pinning are techniques you prefer.

ASSEMBLING THE BLOCKS

You will need the following blocks to make this quilt:

A Block
Make 25.

B Block
Make 24.

C Block
Make 16.

D Block
Make 12.

E Block
Make 4.

Piecing A Blocks

1 Stitch a WGW unit on each side of a Full-Curve unit, nesting seams. Press toward curved block. (Figure 5)

2 Sew a GWGWG unit to the top and to the bottom, nesting seams. Press toward GWGWG units. (Figure 5)

3 Repeat Steps 1–2 until you have a total of 25 A Blocks.

Piecing B Blocks

1 Using FULL SETS ((2) 2″ squares, (2) 5″×2″ strips, and (1) 8″×2″ strip) cut from colored scraps, stitch a BG unit on each side of both 2″ colored squares with the light gray fabric on either side of the colored square. Press seams toward the background fabric.

2 Stitch one gray square to each side of the 5″×2″ colored strip. Press toward the background fabric.

3 Stitch rows together, nesting seams. (Figure 6) Press toward the second and fourth rows.

4 Repeat until you have a total of 24 B Blocks.

Piecing C Blocks

1 Using HALF SETS ((1) 2″ square and (1) 5″×2″ strip) cut from colored scraps, stitch a BG unit on each side of the 2″ colored square with the light gray fabric on either side of the colored square. Press toward the background fabric.

2 Sew a gray square on each side of the 5″×2″ strip (Figure 7). Press toward the background fabric.

3 Sew rows together, nesting seams. Press toward 5″ strip row.

4 Repeat until you have a total of 16 C Blocks.

Piecing D Blocks

1 Sew a white 2″ square on each side of a Half-Curve unit (Figure 8). Press toward curved block.

2 Sew the Half-Curve unit to a GWGWG unit, nesting seams (see D Block key on facing page for orientation). Press toward GWGWG unit.

3 Repeat until you have a total of 12 D Blocks.

Piecing E Blocks

1 Sew a white 2″ square to a quarter-curve unit (Figure 9). Press toward quarter-curve unit. Nest seams and stitch quarter-curve unit to one WG unit (see E Block key on facing page for orientation). Press toward WG unit.

2 Repeat until you have a total of four E Blocks.

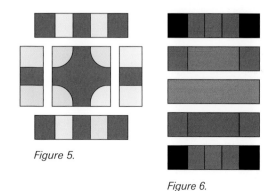

Figure 5.

Figure 6.

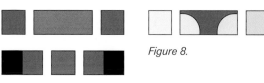

Figure 7.

Figure 8.

Figure 9.

ASSEMBLING THE QUILT TOP

1 Referring to Figure 11, lay out the blocks. Sew blocks together in rows, nesting seams. Press seams in alternating directions: odd rows (first, third, fifth, etc.) to the left and even rows (second, fourth, sixth, etc.) to the right.

2 Nesting seams, pin and sew rows together. Press seams to one side.

3 Piece the 2"×40" the background fabric border strips as needed. Measure, trim, and attach left and right borders. Press toward border. Piece, measure, trim, and attach top and bottom borders.

FINISHING THE QUILT

Layer the quilt top, batting, and backing fabric. Baste, quilt, and bind using your favorite method.

SCRAP STASH TIPS From April Rosenthal

I store my small scraps by color, but larger scraps? I put those together in sizes that coordinate with pre-cut measurements. For example, everything 2½"–4½" I store together, everything from 5"–9½" I store together, and everything larger than 10" stays together, too. Then, when I'm making a project using precut fabrics, I can just pull out that bin and add in additional fabric from my scraps. This helps extend the usefulness of a precut, as well as infuse some variety into the project by incorporating my own combination of scraps.

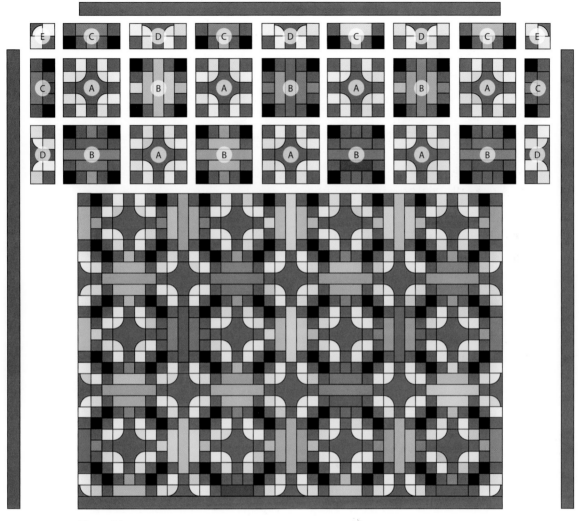

Figure 11.

AUTUMN FLIGHT

By Beth Vassalo

I love the look of the traditional flying geese pattern, but I don't love how I can never seem to keep all the points of the center triangle "pointy." The geese in this project are pieced using improvisational techniques and are "floating" inside a block — making it virtually impossible to lose any points!

I designed this quilt so that it can be pieced either by block or by row. I chose to piece it by row, thus eliminating the need to match any seams in the construction of the entire quilt!

Finished Block Size: 15″×16″

Finished Quilt Size: 58½″×73½″

MATERIALS

Triangle Fabric Scraps: scraps totaling approximately ¾ yard; 27 pieces at least 5'' square

Print Fabric Scraps: scraps totaling approximately 4¼ yards; see chart for minimum scrap size

Background Fabric: 2 yards (or scraps of neutral fabric totaling 2 yards)

Binding Fabric: ½ yard

Backing Fabric: 4 yards

Batting: 65''×80''

Size Requirements for Print Fabric Scraps

Unless otherwise noted, each block needs nine scraps measuring at least the size listed below. When two sizes are listed, you need two scraps from the same fabric — one in each size listed.

Fabric	Approx. Total Yardage	Minimum Scrap Size	Number Needed	Notes
Scrap Pile A	1	9''×9''	9	you may substitute 36 4½'' squares (4 squares of 9 prints)
		6''×7''	9	one of each of the same fabrics from the previous cut
Scrap Pile B	¼	3½''×6''	9	
Scrap Pile C	⅛	2''×7''	9	
Scrap Pile D	¾	5''×5''	27	9 different fabrics, 3 pieces of each
Scrap Pile E	¾	7''×9''	9	
		5''×5''	9	
Scrap Pile F	⅜	4½''×5''	9	
Scrap Pile G	¾	4''×4''	27	9 different fabrics, 3 pieces of each
		5''×6''	9	one of each of the same fabrics from the previous cut
Scrap Pile H	¼	4''×4''	9	
		1½''×5''	9	

CUTTING

Note: Width of Fabric = WOF

From Triangle Fabric, cut:

- (9) 4'' squares
- (9) 4½'' squares
- (9) 5'' squares
- Subcut each square on each the diagonal to make four triangles for a total of 108 triangles. While cutting, organize your triangles into three piles labeled with the size of the original square.

From Scrap Pile A, cut:

- Along the center vertically and horizontally, then across each diagonal, cut the 9'' square to make eight triangles. If you are using the four 4½'' squares, cut each square once on the diagonal. Label the pile.

From Scrap Pile D, cut:

- (27) 5'' squares; subcut each square on the diagonal once to make two triangles for a total of 54 triangles. Label the pile.

From Scrap Pile G, cut:

- (27) 4'' squares; subcut each square on the diagonal once to make two triangles for a total of 54 triangles. Label the pile.

From Background Fabric, cut:

- Lengthwise strips or piece together neutral scraps until you have strips measuring: 3''×46'', 9''×46'', 12½''×59½'', and 17''×59½''

From Binding Fabric, cut:

- (7) 2½'' x WOF strips

QUILTER TO QUILTER

If you have a scrap you want to use in your quilt that isn't quite the measurement listed, you might still be able to use it by slightly adjusting the size of another piece in the same row. Except when specifically noted otherwise, I recommend waiting to trim your scraps until after you have pieced them together. However, note that for the square pieces listed in Scrap Piles A, D, and G, your fabric must be at least the measurement listed.

ASSEMBLING THE BLOCKS

Flying Geese Sets

All seam allowances are ¼'' and all seams are pressed open. Press after each step.

1 Align one triangle from the 4½'' square pile on a triangle from the 9'' square pile, leaving approximately 1'' at the top (Figure 1). Sew.

2 Press and trim.

3 Align the second large triangle on the other side of the center triangle (Figure 2). Sew and press.

4 Repeat using triangles from the same pile until you have four flying geese.

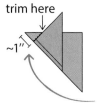

trim here

~1''

Figure 1.

QUILTER TO QUILTER

The 1'' offset does not need to be exact. Measure the first few so that you get an idea of how much of the bottom triangle should be peeking out, but then just estimate for the rest. I use scissors to quickly trim the point from the larger triangle.

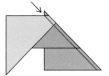

stitch here using ¼'' seam allowance

Figure 2.

SCRAP STASH TIPS From Beth Vassalo

Until I have only a small square or narrow strip left of a fabric, I store the scrap with the larger piece of the matching fabric. Once I have only a small amount left of a particular fabric, I add it to a drawer with the rest of my small scraps. When the drawer starts overflowing, thus motivating me to organize, I like to organize the scraps by size and type. I first separate out the scraps of my most favorite fabrics and keep those together. Next I separate out the novelty prints. And finally, I organize by size into groups of small squares, large squares, and strips.

5 Trim the top and bottom of each flying geese block (Figure 3). When trimming the top of the block, leave between ¼''–¾'' inch between the top point of the triangle and the edge of the block. Vary the amount trimmed at the top of each block to create a random look.

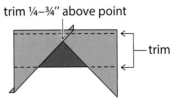

trim ¼–¾'' above point

trim

Figure 3.

6 Determine how you want to lay out the set of four flying geese blocks and trim the sides of each block so they measure 5½'' across (Figure 4). Vary the amount of seam allowance on either side of the triangle, but be sure to always leave at least ¼''.

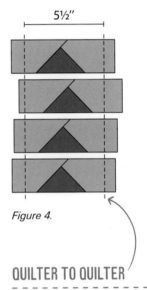

5½''

Figure 4.

7 Repeat Steps 1 through 6 with the rest of the triangles from the 4½'' and 9'' square piles. **This is Set A.** You'll have nine sets of four blocks.

QUILTER TO QUILTER

For Step 6, I like to make the initial cut about ¼'' larger than necessary, and then I trim again to the final measurement after sewing the flying geese blocks together.

8 Repeat Steps 1 through 6 using triangles from the 5'' triangle pile combined with triangles from Scrap Pile D (5'' pile) to make sets of *three* flying geese (not four). Keep the remaining triangles in their labeled piles. (Note: The triangles are both cut from 5'' squares, but the gray squares were cut twice on the diagonal and the print triangles were cut only once so they are significantly larger than the gray triangles.) Trim these sets to 6½''. **This is Set B.** You'll have nine sets of three blocks.

9 Repeat Steps 1 through 6 using triangles from the 4'' triangle pile combined with triangles from Scrap Pile G (4'' pile), again making sets of *three* flying geese. Keep the remaining triangles in their labeled piles. Trim these sets to 4½''. **This is Set C.** You'll have nine sets of three blocks.

Single Flying Geese

1 Cut the 5″ squares from Scrap Pile E in half diagonally. Pair those triangles with the remaining triangles from the 5″ triangle pile to make nine flying geese using the method described on page 64. Trim to 2½″×6½″ (**Single Geese A**).

2 Repeat using the 4″ squares from Scrap Pile H and the remaining triangles from the 4″ triangle pile (Figure 5). Trim to 2¼″×4½″ (**Single Geese B**).

Note: Leave at least ½″ between the top point of the triangle and edge of the block.

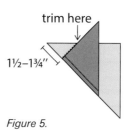

Figure 5.

QUILTER TO QUILTER

When making Single Geese B, I like to leave 1½″–1¾″ of the larger triangle peeking out from below. This gives a larger seam allowance on the top of the triangle (and a smaller one on either side), which makes it easier to keep the point intact when sewing the rows together during the final assembly. Just be sure that there is at least a ¼″ seam allowance on either side of the block.

ASSEMBLING THE ROWS

Block A

1 Referring to Figure 6, pair the flying geese from Set A with the matching 6″×7″ scrap from Scrap Pile A. Trim the shorter edge of the scrap to 5½″ and sew that edge to the left 5½″ edge of the flying geese set. (I like to sew the scrap to the flying geese first and trim second. Decide what works best for you.) Trim to 5½″×14″, being sure to trim the excess from the scrap fabric, not from the flying geese.

2 Sew a piece of fabric from Scrap Pile B to the right of the flying geese set. Trim to 5½″×16½″.

3 Repeat until you have nine blocks.

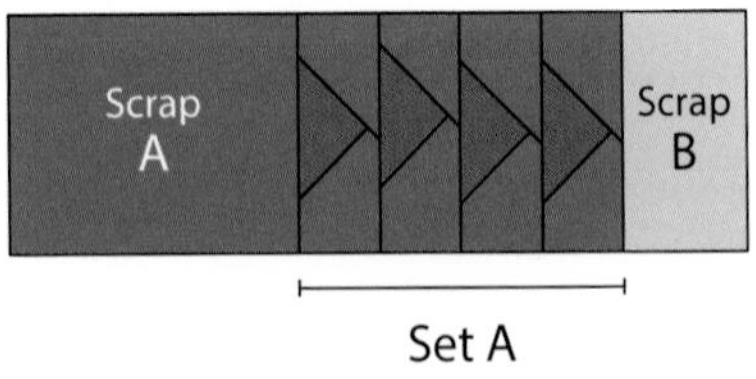

Block B

1 Referring to Figure 7, sew a large scrap from Scrap Pile E to the right of Single Geese A. Trim to 6½″×8″.

2 Sew a flying geese Set B to the left of Single Geese A.

3 Sew a scrap from Scrap pile C to the left of Set B.

4 Trim to 6½″×16½″.

5 Repeat Steps 1 through 4 until you have 9 blocks.

Figure 6.

QUILTER TO QUILTER

For variety, you can wait until the row is complete before trimming so that you can vary the alignment of each row once you see them all together.

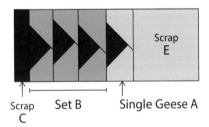

Figure 7.

Block C

1 Referring to Figure 8, pair Single Geese B with the matching small scrap from Scrap Pile H. Sew the scrap to the left of the flying geese. Trim to 3″×4½″.

2 Cut a piece from Scrap Pile G to 2½″×6″. Sew to the left of Scrap H. Sew the remainder of the scrap to the left of Set C. Trim to 4½″×10″.

3 Sew a scrap from scrap Pile F to the bottom of the piece from Step 2 above.

4 Assemble into a row. (Figure 8)

5 Trim to 4½″×16½″.

6 Repeat Steps 1 through 5 until you have nine blocks.

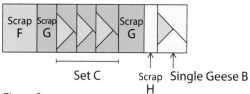

Figure 8.

QUILTER TO QUILTER

To further make use of your scraps, you might consider using neutrals from your scrap stash to build the borders. Simply piece together scraps until you have created the exact size indicated in Adding the Borders (right).

ASSEMBLING THE QUILT TOP

1 Sew three Block As together along the short edge to form Row 1. Press and trim to 5½″×48½″. Repeat to create three Row 1s.

2 Sew three Block Bs together along the short edge to form Row 2. Press and trim to 5½″×48½″. Repeat to create three Row 2s.

3 Sew three Block Cs together along the short edge to form Row 3. Press and trim to 5½″×48½″. Repeat to create three Row 3s.

4 Referencing Figure 10, sew the rows into three Row 1/2/3 Units. Press.

5 Sew the Row Units together. Press.

Adding the Borders

1 Sew the 3″×46″ strip of background fabric to the left side and the 9″×46″ strip to the right side. Press and trim the top and bottom of the border.

2 Sew the 12½″×59½″ strip to the bottom and the 17″×59½″ strip to the top. Press and trim the quilt top to 59″×74″.

FINISHING THE QUILT

Layer the quilt top, batting, and backing fabric. Baste, quilt, and bind using your favorite method.

Row 1 →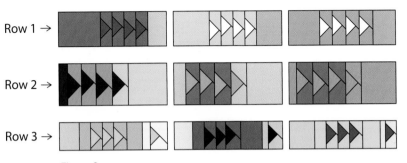

Figure 9.

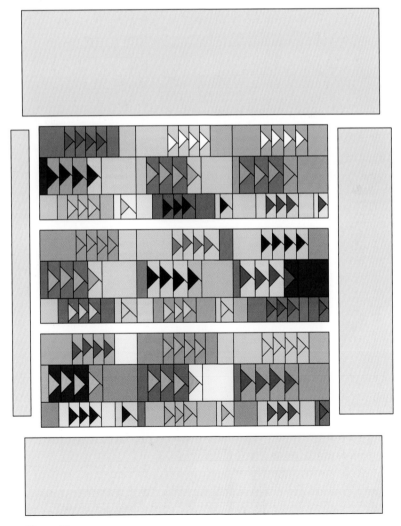

Figure 10.

Project: **8**

Made with
STRIPS+SQUARES

DELIGHTFUL

I have a few fabric scraps that I absolutely treasure. Bits and pieces of favorite fabrics that I've designed, sewn with, or collected, they seemed simply too special to use! This quilt was such a delight for me to make, since I decided it was finally time to make good use of those special scraps. I don't regret it one bit!

By Camille Roskelley

Quilted by
Abby Latimer

Finished Block Size: 12″ square

Finished Quilt Size: 60″×72″

MATERIALS

Scraps: a variety in 2½'' strips and 4½'' squares

Background Fabric: 3 yards

Binding Fabric: ½ yard

Backing Fabric: 3¾ yards

Batting: 66''x 78''

QUILTER TO QUILTER

I love using pre-cuts and always end up with a few bits and pieces at the end of my projects. This is a great project to use up these leftover pieces. My favorite kind of scraps!

CUTTING

Note: Width of Fabric = WOF

From Scraps, cut:
- (27) 4½'' squares for block centers
- (216) 2½''×4½'' rectangles

From Background Fabric, cut:
- (12) 4½''×WOF strips;
  subcut (9) 4½'' squares per strip
  until you have 108
- (14) 2½''×WOF strips;
  subcut (16) 2½'' squares per strip
  until you have 216

- (1) 12½''×WOF strip;
  subcut into (6) 6½''×12½'' rectangles

From Binding Fabric, cut:
- (7) 2½''×WOF strips

ASSEMBLING THE BLOCKS

1 Using a pencil, draw a diagonal line from one corner to the opposite corner on the back of (2) 2½'' background squares. Sew two of the 2½''×4½'' scrappy rectangles together on long side to make one unit. Sew a square in the top left corner of the unit along the pencil line (Figure 1). Trim ¼'' from the seam. Press open. Repeat on the top right corner to complete the unit. Make four units.

Figure 1.

2 Using (4) 4½'' background squares, (1) 4½'' scrappy square, and the units made in Step 1, lay out the blocks (Figure 2). Sew the pieces in three rows of three. Sew the rows together to make one block.

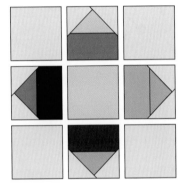

Figure 2.

3 Repeat to make 27 blocks.

QUILTER TO QUILTER

When pressing, I generally press to the dark side and alternate pressing directions on rows. Usually this creates nesting seams automatically, but when it doesn't, I make a special effort to alternate my pressing so my seams will nest whenever they can. A nested seam is a happy seam!

ASSEMBLING THE QUILT TOP

1 Referring to Figure 3, sew blocks together in vertical rows. There are three rows of five blocks and two rows of six blocks.

2 Sew a 12½''×6½'' background rectangle to each end of the 5-block rows.

3 Sew the five rows together to make the quilt top.

FINISHING THE QUILT

Layer the quilt top, batting, and backing fabric. Baste, quilt, and bind using your favorite method.

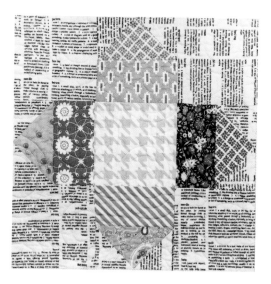

SCRAP STASH TIPS From Camille Roskelley

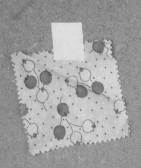

To keep my scraps a bit more organized, I try to divide them into a few different categories: Pre-cut leftovers, less than 5'', and more than 5''. This helps me quickly find the type of scrap I'm looking for. When one of my bins starts to overflow, I either start a new scrappy project or fill up a bag of scraps to send to a quilting friend.

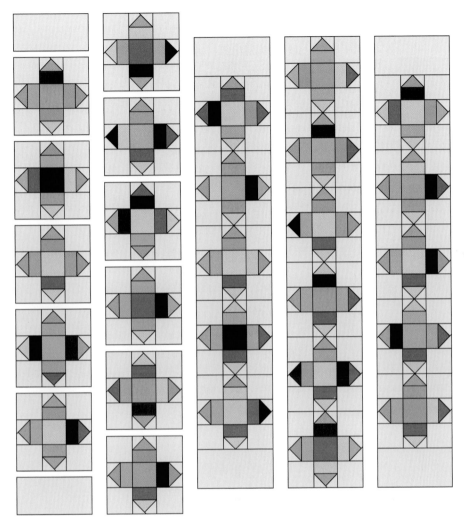

Figure 3.

QUILTER TO QUILTER

When I was playing around with ideas for my quilt, I thought about using the text print for the whole background but decided it was a bit too busy. But I had already made one block, so I decided to include it in my quilt since it brought something fun and scrappy to the mix (see the block opposite). Switching out a background or two is a great way to mix up things in any quilt.

Made with
STRIPS

UNRAVELED

By Faith Jones

Sometimes the simplest designs are the most beautiful. Beginning with a basic element then adding small details invites transformation. For this quilt, I began with 3″ squares. I added small white pops in the opposing corners and laid out the pieced squares to form a ring of prints for each 12″ quilt block. Finally, I turned the blocks on point for added interest. By alternating the blocks with an "empty" square (from the background fabric), an unraveling chain effect was created.

Consider replacing the white background fabric with a darker solid choice and then piecing the block with a scrappy mix of neutrals. Or, consider reversing the background and focal fabrics, using a scrappy mix of bold prints in place of the white and a neutral in place of the prints. The neutral will allow your eye to rest while taking in the variety of other fabrics.

Finished Block Size: 12″ square

Finished Quilt Size: 68″×85″

MATERIALS

Scraps:

- **Fabric A (a variety of purple scraps):** approximately (20) 3½'' strips at least 14'' in length
- **Fabric B (a variety of yellow scraps):** approximately (20) 3½'' strips at least 14'' in length
- **Fabric C (a variety of turquoise scraps):** approximately (20) 3½'' strips at least 14'' in length

Fabric D (background): 4½ yards

Binding Fabric: ⅔ yard

Backing Fabric: 5½ yards

Batting: 74''×91'

CUTTING

Note: Width of Fabric = WOF

From Fabric A, B, and C, cut:

- (80) 3½'' squares each, for a total of 240 squares

From Fabric D, cut:

- (17) 1½''×WOF strips; subcut into (480) 1½'' squares
- (7) 3½''×WOF strips; subcut into (80) 3½'' squares
- (4) 12½''×WOF strips; subcut into (12) 12½'' squares
- (3) 12⅞''×WOF strips; subcut into (7) 12⅞'' squares, then cut diagonally into 14 triangles.
- (1) 13¼'' square; subcut diagonally twice, corner to corner; subcut into four triangles

From Binding Fabric, cut:

- (9) 2½''×WOF strips

Marking Tip

Many tools can be used for marking fabric. Depending on the color and type of my fabric, I prefer Clover Hera markers, Dritz disappearing ink marking pens, or chalk marking tools.

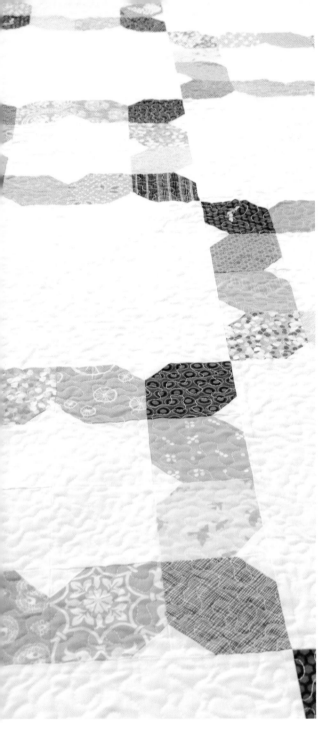

ASSEMBLING THE BLOCKS

1 Using a marking tool, draw a line from corner to corner on all (480) 1½'' Fabric D background squares.

2 Select a 3½'' square from Fabric A. Place a 1½'' white square in one corner. Sew along the marked line.

3 Using a ruler, trim the corner seam allowance to ¼'' (Figure 1). Press.

4 Place another 1½'' white square in the opposite diagonalcorner.

5 Sew along the marked line.

6 Using a ruler, trim the corner seam allowance to ¼'' (Figure 2). Press.

7 Repeat Steps 1–6 for the remaining (239) 3½'' squares in Fabrics A, B, and C.

Figure 1.

Figure 2.

Trimming Tip:
If necessary, use an acrylic ruler to square the pieced block component to 3½''×3½''.

8 Select a 3½″ Fabric D background square and 1 pieced block component from each of your color families for a total of (4) 3½″ squares. Referring to Figure 3, lay out fabric squares.

9 Sew squares together (Figure 3), taking care to match the background fabric to where their seams meet for accraute points. Press.

10 Repeat Steps 8 and 9 to create three additional block quadrants. Lay out block quadrants as indicated in Figure 4.

11 Sew squares together (see Figure 4), taking care again to match the background fabric at the seams. Press to one side.

12 Repeat to create 19 additional 12½″ square blocks, for a total of 20 blocks.

Figure 3.

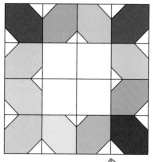

Figure 4.

Piecing Tip:
Place a straight pin at the point where the background seams meet to ensure a perfect match.

ASSEMBLING THE QUILT TOP

1 Referring to Figure 5, lay out the 20 pieced quilt blocks, (12) 12½″ Fabric D white squares, 14 larger Fabric D background triangles, and the 4 smaller Fabric D background triangles on point.

2 Sew the squares together into diagonal strips. Press.

3 Sew the diagonal strips together to complete the quilt top. Press.

FINISHING THE QUILT

Layer the quilt top, batting, and backing fabric. Baste, quilt, and bind using your favorite method.

Figure 5.

 I separate my scraps into three groupings: warm colors (pinks, reds, oranges, and yellows), cool colors (greens, blue, purples, and grays) and solid fabrics. I keep them in wire mesh storage bins, which allows me to easily see around the sides when I'm looking for a particular color or print. As an added bonus, the mesh bins make an attractive addition to the decor in my sewing space.

Made with
SQUARES

SUNSET TILES

By Jeni Baker

Play with color and pattern in your fabric selection using this simple block. I chose a palette of warm pinks and golds, cooled down with teal, and finished off with shots of black and gray. The pop of white unifies and calms the quilt down. The blocks are set on point to add even more interest.

I was inspired by a set of bed sheets I saw on one of my scavenger hunts. I visit my favorite shops and landmarks, on the lookout for interesting colors, patterns, and designs. I quickly sketched the idea and it marinated for a long time before I sat down to design a quilt around it. The colors came together based on a desert sunset. Experiment with color combinations or fussy cut your favorite prints in this versatile quilt packed with movement.

Finished Block Size: 5″ square

Finished Quilt Size: 56½″×77½″

MATERIALS

Scraps: a variety of print scraps at least 4¼''×7¾''

Background Fabric: 1 yard solid neutral fabric

Binding Fabric: ½ yard

Backing Fabric: 3½ yards

Batting: 63''×84''

Example of Scrap Cutting Layout

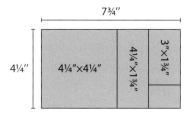

CUTTING

Note: Width of Fabric = WOF

From Scraps, cut:
- (195) 4¼'' squares
- (195) 4¼''×1¾'' strips
- (195) 3''×1¾'' strips

From Background Fabric, cut:
- (7) 1¾''×WOF strips; subcut into (390) 1¾'' squares

From Binding Fabric, cut:
- (7) 2½''×WOF strips

QUILTER TO QUILTER

To achieve good variety in your blocks, I recommend piecing randomly. Put all your scraps into a container and choose them without looking. You will end up with some fun fabric combinations that you might not put together otherwise.

SCRAP STASH TIPS From Jeni Baker

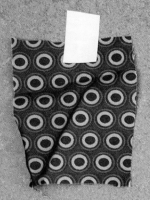

I have tried many different solutions for storing my scraps. What works best for me at the moment is to store scraps by print type. Solid scraps are kept in one bin, blender print scraps in one bin, and general print scraps in a third bin. I do not cut down any of my scraps before they go into the bin. This system works well with the type of projects I make.

ASSEMBLING THE BLOCKS

1 To create a single block, use
(1) 4¼'' square, (1) 4¼''×1¾'' strip,
(1) 3''×1¾'' strip and (2) 1¾''
background squares. You want the
two strips to be the same print.

2 Sew a 1¾'' background square
to one end of the 3''×1¾'' strip.
Press the seam away from the
background square.

3 Sew the unit from Step 2 to the
bottom of the 4¼'' square with the
background square on the right. Press
the seam toward the 4¼'' square.

4 Sew a 1¾'' solid square to one end
of the 4¼''×1¾'' strip. Press the seam
away from the background square.

5 Sew the unit from Step 4 to the left
side of the unit from Step 3. The
background square should be at the
top (Figure 1). Press the seam toward
the 4¼'' square.

6 Repeat Steps 1 through 5 to create
a total of 195 blocks.

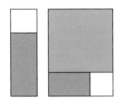

Figure 1.

QUILTER TO QUILTER

When pressing seams in a single
direction, it can be easier to press from
the right side first. Once the seam is
firmly set on the right side, you can flip
it over and press again from the back
to finish it off.

QUILTER TO QUILTER

If you are working with a ton of colors,
focus on each block as its own individual
color palette. This can establish a little
rhyme and reason to what otherwise
could become a crazy color composition!

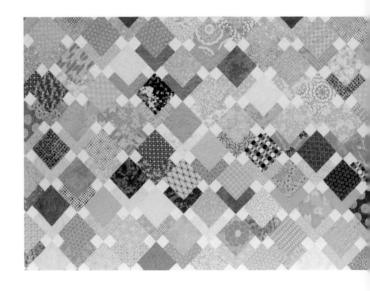

Figure 2.

QUILTER TO QUILTER

Label each row with a numbered marker, such as a small slip of paper, to keep things organized. This is especially helpful when sewing blocks on point.

ASSEMBLING THE QUILT TOP

1 In order to arrange the blocks on point, the rows will be attached diagonally. Each row varies in size. The shortest rows are the top left and bottom right corners, and the longest rows are in the middle. Refer to Figure 2 for the number of blocks in each diagonal row. Starting at the top left corner, stitch together the blocks in each diagonal row. Press the seams to opposite sides in each row to ensure the seams nest nicely.

2 Follow Figure 2 closely when lining up your rows aligning the strips. Sew rows together, starting from the top left corner and working down toward the bottom right corner. Press the seams open. (Press the quilt top well from the right side, using spray starch or a spray starch alternative to reduce the possibility of stretching.)

3 To trim the quilt top, it is helpful to work on a large table or on the floor. Beginning with the right edge of the quilt top, locate the right points of the background squares at the bottom right edge. Using an acrylic ruler and a cutting mat, measure ¼'' to the right of the points and cut away the excess fabric. Continue to line up the ruler against the background squares, ensuring the quilt top is straight. Work along one side, then turn the corner and continue until the entire quilt top has been trimmed.

Figure 3.

FINISHING THE QUILT

Layer the quilt top, batting, and backing fabric. Baste, quilt, and bind using your favorite method.

WOVEN

**By Kati
Spencer**

*Quilted by
Barbie Mills*

This pattern is a fresh take on a smaller project
I created several years ago. I love the simple lines
of the blocks. The color palette I chose is a current
favorite of mine: navy, coral, red, and golden
yellow mixed with several neutrals and a textured
neutral background fabric. When selecting fabrics
for this quilt, begin with five to eight fairly specific
colors. Search for new color inspiration — I love
finding new potential color combos in displays at
some of my favorite shops, paint swatches at a
home store, or the websites that pull colors from
inspirational photos. Solids and tone-on-tone
fabrics work best for this project. These fabrics
allow the block design to pop, emphasizing the
distinct lines of the strips in the blocks.

Finished Block Size: 20″ square

Finished Quilt Size: 72″ x72″

MATERIALS

Scraps: approximately 4½ yards of a variety of strips in desired colors

Background Fabric: 2⅛ yards

Backing Fabric: 4½ yards

Binding Fabric: ½ yard

Batting: 78"×78"

QUILTER TO QUILTER

If you do not have enough scrappy strips to create this quilt, fat eighths work well for this project. Approximately thirty-six fat eighths are needed. Alternately eighteen fat quarters could be used, but would offer less variation of color and design.

CUTTING

Note: Width of Fabric = WOF

From Scraps, cut:

- (27) 2"×20½" strips
- (45) 1¾"×20½" strips
- (45) 1½"×20½" strips
- (27) 1¼"×20½" strips
- (27) 1"×20½" strips
- (18) ¾"×20½" strips

Join two or more short strips of the same height to create scrappy strips. Press seams open and trim to the required 20½" length. Keep strips separated by measurements for ease when sorting strips for blocks.

From Background Fabric, cut:

- (2) 4½"×72½" strips
- (2) 4½"×64½" strips
- (2) 2½"×64½" strips
- (6) 2½"×20½" strips

From Binding Fabric, cut:

- (7) 2½"×WOF strips

QUILTER TO QUILTER

To keep all the scraps organized, I stored the required scraps for each block in separate sandwich-size plastic bags. Sew each block one at a time to minimize confusion.

Background Cutting Diagram

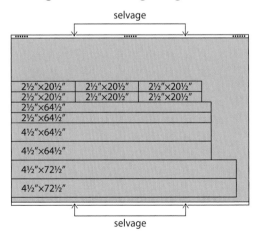

ASSEMBLING THE BLOCKS

1 Divide fabric strips for blocks. Each block requires (3) 2'' strips, (5) 1¾'' strips, (5) 1½'' strips, (3) 1¼'' strips, (3) 1'' strips, and (2) ¾'' strips.

2 Randomly cut and arrange block strips. Pin and sew in pairs. Backstitch at the beginning and end of each seam. Press seams. Join pairs and press, repeating until all strips are joined into the block. Be sure to leave a few stips going across the full length of the block for interest. (Figure 1)

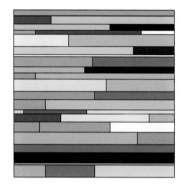

Figure 1.

QUILTER TO QUILTER

Due to the number of seams on each block, a scant ¼'' seam allowance is very important. If a completed block turns out shorter than the required 20½'', you can easily add an additional strip to the top or bottom. Press and trim to 20½''.

Ironing Tip

Carefully press seams open on these strip blocks to create straight, even seams. Pressing to the side may skew the appearance, especially on the ¼'' finished strips.

ASSEMBLING THE QUILT TOP

1 Referring to Figure 2, join blocks in sets of three with the 2½"×20½" background strips in between each block. Press seams toward background fabric. Be sure to alternate the rotation of blocks to create a woven appearance. Repeat with each row.

2 Sew the rows together with the 2½"×64½" background strips of in between each row. Press seams toward background fabric.

3 Attach borders to the sides using the 4½"×64½" background strips. Press seams toward borders. Finish quilt top by adding the 4½"×72½" background strips on top and bottom. Press seams toward borders.

FINISHING THE QUILT

Layer the quilt top, batting, and backing fabric. Baste, quilt, and bind using your favorite method.

QUILTER TO QUILTER

Don't hesitate to adjust block size as needed for alternate designs using this strip block. My original version of this project was a 17"×40" table runner.

Project 11: Woven

Figure 2.

SCRAP STASH TIPS From Kati Spencer

I've used various methods for storing scraps, but my current favorite is the Trofast system from the IKEA children's department. The bins are just the right size and slide out for easy sorting. I sort scraps by color and create vinyl bin labels in corresponding colors to keep everything organized.

When I have strips of fabric remaining after a project, I store those separately and save them for another strings quilt down the road. Scrap strips that measure 2½'' are also stored separately. I save those for scrappy bindings, like the binding on my project here.

Made with
SQUARES

FIRE WHIRL

By Lee Heinrich

When I think scrap quilts, I think busy, I think colorful, and I think of lots of small pieces. Fire Whirl has all of that, but instead of randomly scattering color across the quilt, colored half-square triangles are carefully placed to give the feeling of wheels of fire. Because there are so many half-square triangles (HSTs) needed to make this quilt, I've provided a quick method that uses paper piecing. Use my template (page 127) to easily create eight HSTs at one time! You will still have to do some trimming, but it's not nearly as painstaking as squaring up each HST individually. All you need are some larger scraps.

Finished Block Size: 10″ square
Finished Quilt Size: 60″×80″

MATERIALS

Scraps (a variety of fabrics in two color groupings):
- Dark yellow, light yellow, dark emerald, light emerald, dark purple, and light purple scraps: totaling approximately ¼ yard for each color
- Teal, royal blue, navy, yellow-orange, medium orange, and dark orange scraps: totaling approximately ½ yard for each color

Background Fabric: 4¼ yards

Binding Fabric: ½ yard

Backing Fabric: 5 yards

Batting: 66''×86''

CUTTING

Note: Width of Fabric = WOF

From Dark Yellow, Light Yellow, Dark Emerald, and Light Emerald Scraps, cut:
- (3) 6¼''×8½'' rectangles of each color

From Dark Purple and Light Purple Scraps, cut:
- (6) 6¼''×8½'' rectangles of each color

From Teal, Royal Blue, Navy, Yellow-Orange, Medium Orange, and Dark Orange Scraps, cut:
- (12) 6¼''×8½'' rectangles of each color

From Background Fabric, cut:
- (96) 6¼''×8½'' pieces

From Binding Fabric, cut:
- (7) 2½''×WOF strips

SCRAP STASH TIPS From Lee Heinrich

When it comes to storing scraps, I think it's hard to beat the basic clear plastic shoe box. These containers are available from big box stores for less than $2 apiece — I have a box for every spot on the color wheel. They're very stackable and storable, and because they're clear, it's easy to see exactly which box you need to pull from when you're looking for scraps in a certain color. And they still look pretty on your shelves!

MAKING THE HALF-SQUARE TRIANGLES (HSTs)

1 Make 96 copies of the half-square triangle template on page 127. Cut out the templates on the outer solid line. Pair up colored scrap pieces with gray (background) pieces, right sides together. Place a copy of the template on top of each gray/colored pair. The wrong side of one of the pieces of fabric should face the wrong (unprinted) side of the template. The edges of the fabric should approximately line up with the edges of the paper template. Pin into place.

2 Sew through the template and both layers of fabric on the angled dotted lines.

3 Cut on the solid black lines to create HSTs. Remove the paper. Press seams open.

QUILTER TO QUILTER

There is no need to be exact when cutting out the half-square triangle templates. You'll be trimming again on the solid lines after sewing. Also, lower your stitch length to between 1.4mm and 1.6mm when sewing through the paper templates. This will help perforate the paper, allowing you to remove it more easily later.

You will need the following HST units to make this quilt:

 24
light yellow/background fabric

 24
dark yellow/background fabric

 24
light emerald/background fabric

 24
dark emerald/background fabric

 48
light purple/background fabric

 48
dark purple/background fabric

 96
teal/background fabric

 96
royal blue/background fabric

 96
navy blue/background fabric

 96
yellow-orange/background fabric

 96
medium orange/background fabric

 96
dark orange/background fabric

ASSEMBLING THE BLOCKS

Sew HST units together (Figure 1), paying close attention to the color placements in each block. Press all seams open.

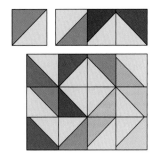

Figure 1.

ASSEMBLING THE QUILT TOP

1 Rotating each block 90 degrees (Figure 2), make groups of four blocks that form the "fire whirl" design, with the yellow and orange whirl at the center of the 4-block groups, as shown.

2 Starting at the top left corner, stitch together the groups into four blocks (Figure 2), pressing all seams open.

3 Sew the 4-block groups together into four rows of three 4-block groups each. Press seams open. Combine the rows to complete the quilt top (Figure 2).

FINISHING THE QUILT

Layer the quilt top, batting, and backing fabric. Baste, quilt, and bind using your favorite method.

QUILTER TO QUILTER

I highly recommend pressing all seams open in this quilt. With so many seams coming together in so many different directions, pressing seams open will greatly reduce seam bulk and allow for much easier seam matching.

Figure 2.

DIAMONDS
IN THE SKY

By Melissa Lunden

This gorgeous oversized throw quilt is perfect for using up scraps in a modern and minimalist way. The deconstructed blocks create classic chevrons and diamonds, which work with any decor. Pair and piece your scraps by color and then highlight them with a white background. This project uses easy strip piecing construction that will ensure perfect diagonal seams for your blocks. Templates are then cut from the scrap strips and sewn into blocks, making it an ideal scrap buster.

I chose scraps from my favorite color palate of aqua, turquoise, gray, green, and a fun pop of magenta. Pick an inspirational color story, pull coordinating fabrics from your stash, and get to work.

Finished Block Size: 8″×12″

Finished Quilt Size: 64½″×66½″

MATERIALS

Scraps: 4½ yards total of at least 20 coordinating prints cut into 3¼″×19″ pieces; see below for tips on how to use smaller scraps

Background Fabric: 3½ yards

Binding Fabric: ½ yard

Backing Fabric: 4 yards

Batting: 70″×72″

How to Use Smaller Scraps:

If you have shorter scraps, the 3¼″-wide strips can be a minimum of 7″ in length. A pair of 7″ strips will be enough for one template piece. A pair of 3¼″×13″ strips will be enough for two template pieces. One pair of 3¼″×19″ strips will be enough for three template pieces. If you are working with 7″ or 13″ pieces, be sure to have equal numbers of each size. You need to have enough pairs of scraps to make a total of 140 total template pieces.

CUTTING

Note: Width of Fabric = WOF

From Scraps, cut:

- (94) 3¼″×19″ strips (sort them into two piles including a nice variety of each color; these strips will be paired with a strip of background fabric to make a strip set)

From Background Fabric, cut:

- (47) 19″×1⅞″ strips for the strip sets (If you are working with smaller pieces, cut the background strips to match the length of your scrap strips, either 7″×1⅞″ or 13″×1⅞″. Cut one background strip for every pair of scrap strips you have.)
- (70) 6″×1½″ strips
- (35) 8½″×1½″ strips
- (40) 12½″×1½″ strips for vertical sashing
- (18) 1½″×WOF strips for horizontal sashing; subcut six strips in half

From Binding Fabric, cut:

- (7) 2½″×WOF strips

QUILTER TO QUILTER

I recommend pressing your seams open, especially with thicker fabrics like linen (which I used). If you don't like that technique or if you find some of the seams to be too bulky, press your seams toward the darker prints. Otherwise, the darker print might show through the white sashing.

BLOCK PREPARATION

1 Creating the Strip Sets: Each strip set consists of a 3¼''-wide strip of prints sewn to either side of a 1⅞''-wide center strip of white fabric (Figure 1). Create 47 strip sets 19'' long from your piles of scrap strips. If using shorter strips, you'll need 140 strip sets from 7'' long strips or 70 strip sets from 13'' long strips. Press.

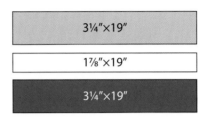

Figure 1.

2 Making the Templates: To make Templates A and B, first draw a pair of 4''×6'' rectangles on white paper. Mark the 2'' and 4'' points on the 6'' sides. To make Template A, draw a diagonal line from the 2'' line on one side of the rectangle to the opposite top corner; then draw a parallel line from the bottom corner to the 4'' mark on the opposite corner. Make three copies. Repeat for Template B, drawing the diagonal lines in the opposite direction. Be sure label each template (Figure 2).

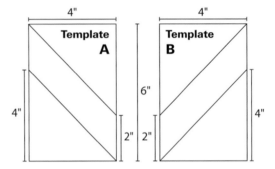

Figure 2.

3 Cutting the Templates: To use the templates, place it on one edge of a strip set. Line up the diagonal lines of the template with the seams (Figure 3). You can cut three rectangles from one 19'' strip.

The top of the bottom scrap piece should line up exactly with the bottom diagonal line of the template. Cut 70 from both Template A and B (140 total). Keep the groups separate.

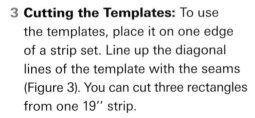

Figure 3.

ASSEMBLING THE BLOCKS

1 Referring to Figure 4, arrange your rectangles to create a nice balance of colors and prints. Each block is made up of 2 rectangle A pieces and 2 rectangle B pieces, plus (2) 6''×1½'' strips and (1) 8½''×1½'' strip.

2 Sew a rectangle A piece to a 6'' sashing piece.

3 Sew a rectangle B piece to the other side of the sashing.

4 Repeat Steps 2 and 3 with the bottom pair of rectangle A and B pieces. Be sure to flip the bottom pair upside down so you create an 'X' with the sashing pieces. (Figure 4)

5 Sew the top rectangle A and B pieces together with the 8½''×1½'' strip.

6 Sew the bottom rectangle A and B pieces to the unit from Step 5.

7 Square up the block to 8½''×12½'' if necessary.

8 Repeat Steps 1 through 7 for the remaining blocks.

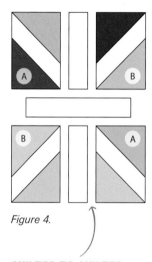

Figure 4.

QUILTER TO QUILTER

Use a little extra care when sewing the background fabric to the template pieces. The center strips are cut on the bias and can stretch very easily. For extra stability, pin the 6'' sashing strips at the ends and center, which will help keep the template pieces the right height.

QUILTER TO QUILTER:

Changing the Size of the Quilt:
The finished block is 8″×12″. Keep these measurements in mind if you want to make a version of this quilt in a different size. Reduce the rows and columns to make a crib quilt or add extra blocks to make a quilt for any size bed in your home. To determine the new size, add 8″ plus 1″ (for each piece of sashing) for each column and 12″ plus 1″ for each row. Be sure to increase the size of your batting and backing to be at least 6″ longer and wider than your finished quilt top.

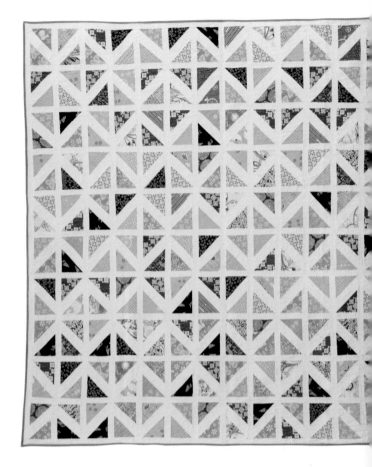

SCRAP STASH TIPS From Melissa Lunden

I keep a large bag next to my cutting table and toss all my small scraps in it as I work on a project. I use these scraps for later projects — and they are perfect when I need to experiment on a new design idea and don't want to cut into my good fabric. For my larger scrap pieces, I keep my scraps sorted by prints and solids.

ASSEMBLING THE QUILT TOP

1 Referring to Figure 5, sew eight vertical sashing pieces between the seven blocks in each row and on either end of the row. Press seams open.

2 Sew each of the 12 WOF horizontal sashing strips together with one of the half cuts to create (12) 65''×1½'' strips. Press seams open.

3 Sew the horizontal sashing strips between the rows of the blocks.

Press seams open as you work. Attach five rows together, adding a sashing strip at the top and bottom. Press seams open.

4 Press the entire top and trim excess horizontal sashing strips as necessary.

FINISHING THE QUILT

Layer the quilt top, batting, and backing fabric. Baste, quilt, and bind using your favorite method.

Project 13: Diamonds in the Sky

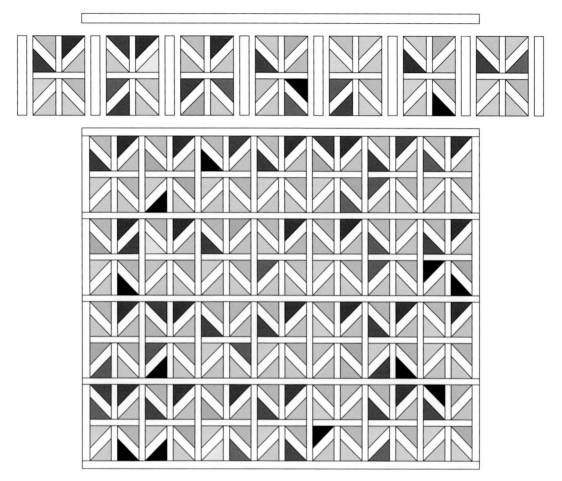

Figure 5.

RICHMOND

By Sherri McConnell

Quilted by Natalia Bonner

I've always loved the Ohio star block and have experimented with it in various arrangements and alternate colorings in several of my quilts. This block lends itself wonderfully to scrap quilts, too. A Quarter-Square Triangle (QST) can be made with small pieces, and block centers need not match the QST sections. This is also the perfect project to use those "I love it so much I can't bear to use it!" fabrics that we as quilters seem to accumulate. It was almost liberating to finally use some of these beautiful prints in a quilt and see them finally brought to life.

Finished Block Size: 9″ square

Finished Quilt Size: 72″×86″

MATERIALS

Scraps:
- **Fabric A:** gray background solid or small print for blocks, sashing, and setting triangles: 5 yards (this can be made up of a combination of fabrics)
- **Fabric B:** white or contrast light fabric for blocks: ⅞ yard
- **Fabric C:** print scraps for block centers: (50) 3½'' squares
- **Fabric D:** print scraps for quarter-square triangles: (100) 4½'' squares (my quilt uses 50 pairs of two matching squares)
- **Fabric E:** scraps for sashing posts: (71) 1½'' squares

Binding Fabric: ¾ yard

Backing Fabric: 5½ yards

Batting: 78''×92''

QUILTER TO QUILTER

Scrap quilts can be daunting for quilters worried about getting just the right mix of fabrics. Don't be afraid to use pieces that don't exactly "go" together in a scrap quilt: It is this kind of an arrangement that gives scrap quilts their character. If you are particularly concerned about whether some pieces are "working" in your quilt, try taking a photograph and viewing the project from a different perspective.

CUTTING

Note: Width of Fabric = WOF

From Fabric A, cut:
- (6) 4½''×WOF strips; subcut into (50) 4½'' squares for QST sections
- (30) 1½''×WOF strips; subcut into (120) 1½''×9½'' sashing rectangles
- (17) 3½''×WOF strips; subcut into (200) 3½'' squares (12 per strip)
- (5) 17'' squares; subcut each square in half diagonally twice for 18 side setting triangles (you will have two triangles left over)
- (2) 9'' squares; subcut each square in half diagonally once for four corner triangles

From Fabric B, cut:
- (6) 4½''×WOF strips; subcut into (50) 4½'' squares for QST sections

From Fabric C, cut:
- (50) 3½'' squares for block centers

From Fabric D, cut:
- (100) 4½'' squares for QST sections (may be in 50 matching pairs or completely scrappy)

From leftover C and D Fabrics (or from additional scraps), cut:
- (71) 1½'' squares for sashing posts

From Binding Fabric, cut:
- (10) 2½''×WOF strips

MAKING THE QUARTER-SQUARE TRIANGLES (QSTs)

1 Referring to page 9 for creating HST units, place a Fabric A 4½'' square and a Fabric D 4½'' square right sides together. Draw a diagonal line on the wrong side of the Fabric A square. Sew ¼'' on either side of the drawn line.

2 Cut on the line and press each resulting HST toward Fabric A.

3 Pair remaining Fabric A squares with Fabric D squares and repeat Steps 1 and 2, to create a total of 100 HST Fabric A/D units.

4 Repeat Steps 1 through 3 with the 50 Fabric B 4½'' squares and the remaining 50 Fabric D 4½'' squares, pressing toward Fabric D, to create a total of 100 HST Fabric B/D units.

5 To make quarter-square triangle (QST) units, place a Fabric A/D HST and a Fabric B/D HST unit right sides together with the diagonal seams nesting (Figure 1). Draw a diagonal line perpendicular to the seam allowance on the wrong side. Sew ¼'' on either side of this line and cut along the drawn line. (Figure 2) Press the seams of each resulting QST to one side.

6 Repeat with remaining HST units to make 200 QST units.

7 Trim all QST units to measure 3½'' square. (Figure 3)

Figure 1.   *Figure 2.*   *Figure 3.*

ASSEMBLING THE BLOCKS

1 Use a 3½'' center square, four quarter-square triangle units, and four Fabric A 3½'' squares to assemble the block units in three rows of three blocks each as shown in Figure 4.

2 Press blocks in each row toward the solid units.

3 Repeat for all 50 scrappy Ohio star blocks.

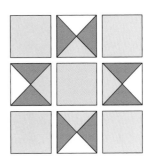

Figure 4.

SCRAP STASH TIPS From Sherri McConnell

I've used a variety of storage methods over the years. What I've finally decided is that the container you use for storage doesn't matter nearly as much as having the scraps cut into useable pieces. I try to be consistent in cutting up leftovers from each project as soon as I'm finished so that my scraps don't amass into an overwhelming group; however, I do keep a bin of fabric to cut later, and when it gets full I take an afternoon to work on "scrap management."

I store 2½'' strips, 2½'' squares, 3½'' squares, and 5'' squares in plastic bins. Because I have eclectic tastes and love soft, traditional fabrics as much as modern brights, I have separated the strips and squares into two collections of each depending on the feel of the fabric. I also store my fat quarters and larger pieces by color on shelves in my sewing room.

QUILTER TO QUILTER

Setting together an on-point quilt can be intimidating. There are a few simple things to do to help make sure you have success with this type of setting. First of all, pin at seam intersections. This simple step helps keep things lined up correctly. Handle your side setting and corner triangles carefully, as they have bias edges that will stretch. Finally, laying out the entire quilt either on a design wall or on a bed or the floor helps to prevent assembly mistakes.

ASSEMBLING THE QUILT TOP

1 Lay out the blocks on point in a pleasing arrangement. Place the 120 sashing strips and 71 post squares (Figure 5). Arrange side setting triangles and corner triangles.

2 Sew the blocks and sashing strips together in rows, beginning and ending each block row with a sashing strip. Press toward the sashing.

3 Add the side setting triangles to the ends of the rows. Press toward the sashing strips.

4 Sew the sashing and post rows together, beginning and ending each of these rows with a post square. Press toward the sashing rectangles.

5 Sew the post/sashing rows to the block rows. Press toward the sashing rectangles.

6 Sew rows together. Press the seams toward the sashing/post rows.

7 Add the corner triangle sections last. Press the seams toward the corner triangles.

8 Trim the quilt top using a 24" acrylic ruler. Be sure to leave ¼" on the outer side of each post so that no corners are cut off when the binding is attached.

9 Stay stitch around the outer edge of the entire quilt to prevent stretching and fraying and to keep seams together. To stay stitch, use a straight stitch and sew a scant ⅛" around the entire quilt.

FINISHING THE QUILT

Layer the quilt top, batting, and backing fabric. Baste, quilt, and bind using your favorite method.

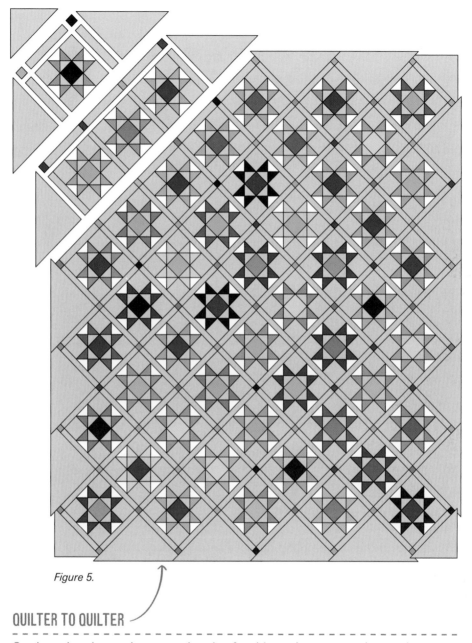

Figure 5.

QUILTER TO QUILTER

Setting triangles and corner triangles for this project are cut larger than necessary to allow for trimming. It's much easier to trim something down to the correct size than to fix something that ended up a bit too small. This method will allow you to create a quilt without any of the points cut off.

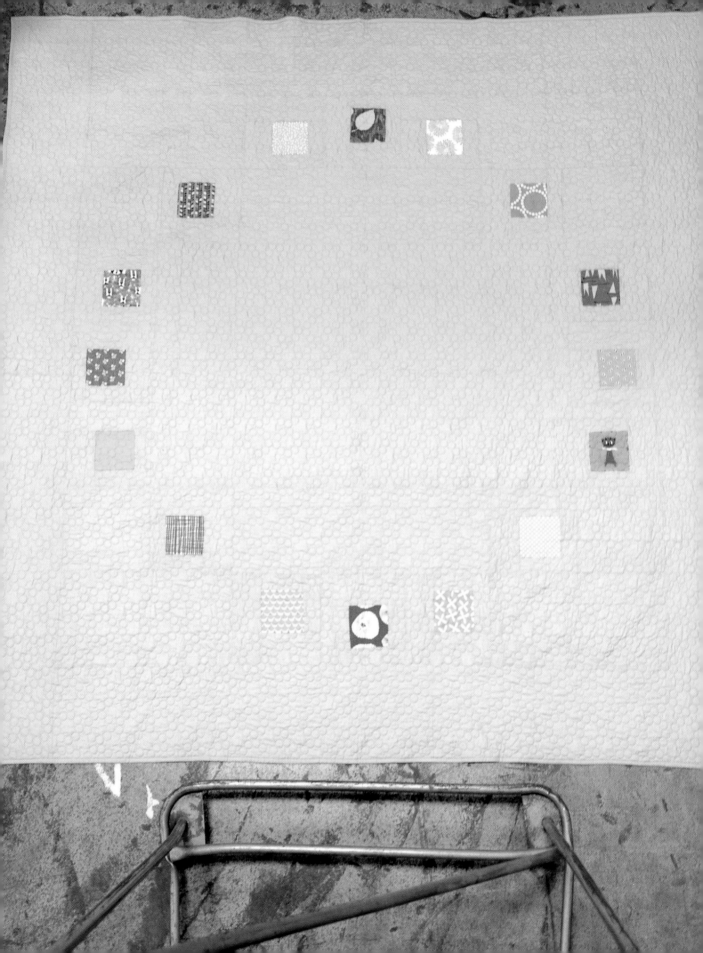

HARVEST GOLD CHARM BRACELET

By Susan Beal

Quilted by Nancy Stovall

This simple, minimal design takes 16 of your favorite scrappy charm squares in a weighted log cabin block setting, and spins them into a "bracelet" design. A curved row of three block center "charms," each rotated differently, connects to the next set diagonally, creating a remarkable circular feel using only straight-line piecing.

Use any bright, dark, or muddy hues for pops of color against a quieter background. I mixed vintage prints in the colors of my own 1970s childhood — avocado green, burnt orange, and of course harvest gold — and combined them with modern fabrics from my scrap boxes. Surrounding them in serene gray lets the colors really shine. Use the precious scraps you've saved from favorite past projects, or organize a charm squares swap for a memorable, modern take on the album quilt.

Finished Block Size: 10″ square

Finished Quilt Size: 90″×90″

MATERIALS

Charm Bracelet Squares:

16 assorted prints, each at least 5″ square

Background Fabric: 5½ yards

Binding Fabric: ¾ yard

Backing Fabric: 8 yards

Batting: 96″×96″

QUILTER TO QUILTER

Before you get started, here are a couple helpful tips:

- Trim all selvages when cutting fabrics.
- Piece all log cabin blocks clockwise and press seams away from centers.

CUTTING

Note: Width of Fabric = WOF

From Assorted Charm Square Fabrics, cut:

- (16) 5″ squares

From Background Fabric, cut:

- (5) 2½″×WOF strips
- (7) 4″×WOF strips
- (8) 10½″×WOF strips; subcut (4) 20½″×10½″ rectangles and (2) 30½″×10½″ rectangles (leave the other 10½″-wide strips uncut for now)
- (1) 50½″×WOF section; subcut (1) 50½″×30½″ rectangle
- (4) 10½″×WOF squares from the remaining fabric

From Binding Fabric, cut:

- (10) 2½″×WOF strips

Choosing Your Charm Squares

The focus fabrics you choose for your charms will add a lot of definition and movement to your quilt, since the bracelet design is so simple. Pull scraps in a larger variety of colors or styles to start with, if you like, and then narrow them down to one or a few that set the tone nicely.

ASSEMBLING THE BLOCKS

1 Design the "bracelet" by laying out 16 charm squares in a circle on a design wall or floor. When you are happy with the layout, take a photo for reference.

2 Chain piece the first 2½" strip of background fabric to the charm squares. Trim between each unit. Press the seams away from the charm squares.

3 Add the second 2½" log the same way as Step 2. Piece clockwise as shown in Figure 1. Trim and press seams away from center.

4 To add the third log, chain piece two-log blocks to a 4" strip of fabric, always piece clockwise. Trim and press away from center. Piece the fourth log in the same way, always piece clockwise and press the seams away from the center.

5 Press your finished blocks back and front. Square blocks so they measure 10½" square. (Figure 1)

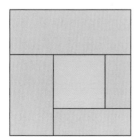

Figure 1.

Directional Charm Squares

If you are working with any directional prints, make a note of exactly where they are placed in the bracelet circle. Using the charm bracelet layout, make a note of how the blocks are oriented and especially which side the first (shortest) narrower log is on, in relation to the center square. Because you rotate your blocks to create the curved "circle" within the pattern, the first log placement varies by charm position.

For example, I wanted to make sure that my cat's head was at the top of my overall block, so I added my first narrower log at the bottom of the center. Mark the first-log side of your center square with a pin or another mark and be sure to stitch your first log there, then continue piecing clockwise as usual from there. After sewing your 16 blocks and laying them out to assemble the quilt top, if you realize that any directional centers are not oriented correctly for the overall pattern, just carefully seam-rip the logs from the center and re-piece them the desired way.

ASSEMBLING THE QUILT TOP

1 Lay out the "bracelet," orienting each one of your blocks (Figure 2) to create the curves of the circle. Press all the subcuts of your background fabric, then use Figure 2 to begin placing them in the right spots in each of the five rows to lay out your quilt.

2 Join Row 1 left to right: a 20½"-wide section, the top set of three blocks, and another 20½"-wide section. Press front and back with seams to the left.

3 Join Row 2 left to right: a 10½" square, a charm block, a 30½"-wide section, a charm block, and a 10½" square. Press, this time with seams to the right.

4 Join Row 3 (the largest row, which comprises the center area of the quilt top) in a few stages. First, join the left side set of three blocks together, press and label it in the upper-left corner, and repeat with the right side set of three blocks. When those sections are prepared, stitch them to the short sides of the 50½"×30½" center piece. Press, with seams to the left.

5 Join Row 4 as you did Row 2, being careful of your block orientation (this row will mirror Row 2 rather than duplicate it), and press with seams to the right.

6 Finally, join Row 5 as you did Row 1, being mindful of your block orientation (this row will mirror Row 1), and press with seams to the left.

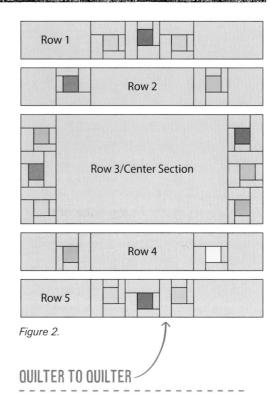

Figure 2.

QUILTER TO QUILTER

Make sure to label the rows as you go. I suggest pinning a small piece of paper with the row number written on it to the upper left-hand corner of the row.

7 Pin the bottom edge of Row 1 to the top edge of Row 2, right sides together. Match seams so that they nest nicely. Stitch together and press the long seam.

8 Now pin the bottom edge of Row 2 to the top edge of Row 3, matching seams. Stitch and press, then set aside for now.

9 Pin the bottom edge of Row 4 to the top edge of Row 5. Stitch and press.

10 Carefully pin the bottom edge of the larger section to the top edge of the smaller section, matching seams. Using a chair or your sewing table to bear the weight of the quilt top, stitch and press the final seam. You have finished the heart of your quilt top!

11 To create borders, join end-to-end the 10½'' background strips you cut earlier to make (2) 70½''×10½'' borders and (2) 90½''×10½'' borders. Stitch a 70½'' border to the top and bottom of the quilt, pressing front and back, and then stitch a 90½'' border to the left and right side of your quilt. Press.

FINISHING THE QUILT

Layer the quilt top, batting, and backing fabric. Baste, quilt, and bind using your favorite method.

SCRAP STASH TIPS From Susan Beal

I organize my fabric in a few different ways. I fold all my larger pieces, ½ yard or over, onto acid-free comic book cardboards (a technique I originally learned from Angela of Cut To Pieces), and keep them in rainbow color order on Ikea Expedit shelves. I fold my FQs or other medium-sized pieces horizontally and stack them, arranged by color too — same with charm squares like the ones I used for my Charm Bracelet quilt.

I also have three pull-out boxes for large scraps divided into warms, cools, and neutrals. I color-copied a favorite piece of vintage fabric in each of these color families and covered each box with that colorful paper, so I know which is which.

My pre-cut or left over fabric strips are all tucked into the biggest drawer of the vintage desk I use as a sewing table, perfect to reach over and grab for improvisational patchwork.

THE TEMPLATES

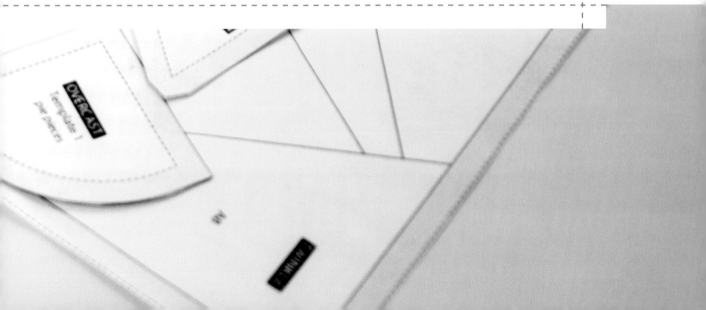

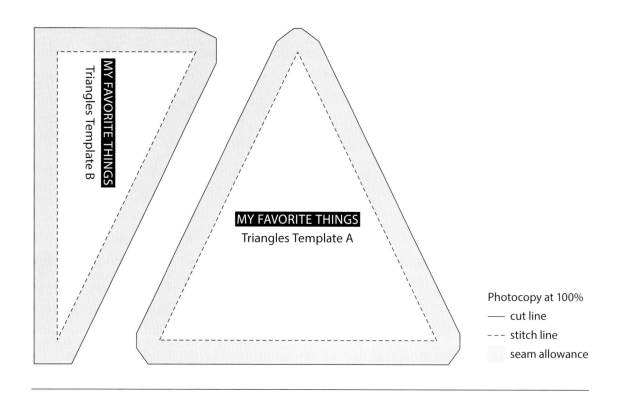

MY FAVORITE THINGS
Triangles Template B

MY FAVORITE THINGS
Triangles Template A

Photocopy at 100%
—— cut line
- - - stitch line
seam allowance

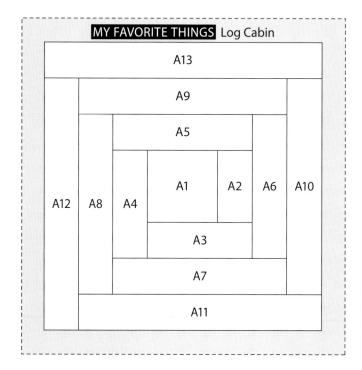

MY FAVORITE THINGS Log Cabin

| A13 |
| A9 |
| A5 |

A12 | A8 | A4 | A1 | A2 | A6 | A10

A3

A7

A11

Photocopy at 100%
- - - cut line
—— stitch line
seam allowance

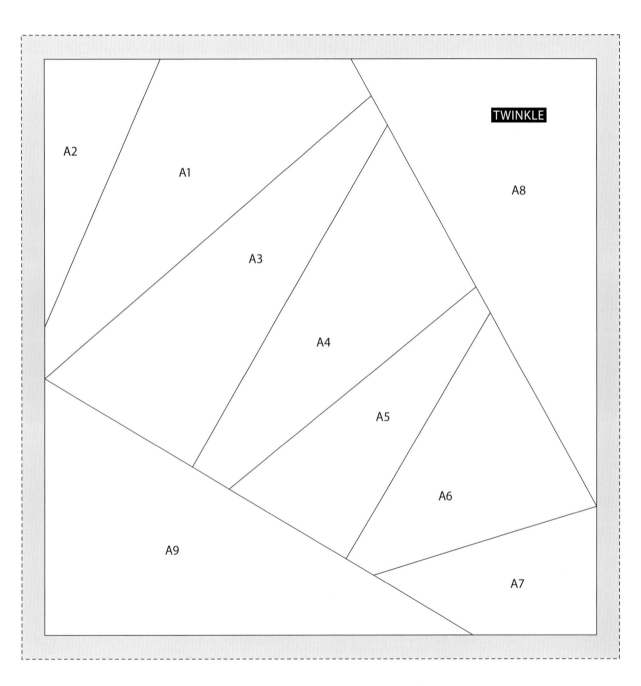

Photocopy at 100%

- - - cut line

—— stitch line

▨ seam allowance

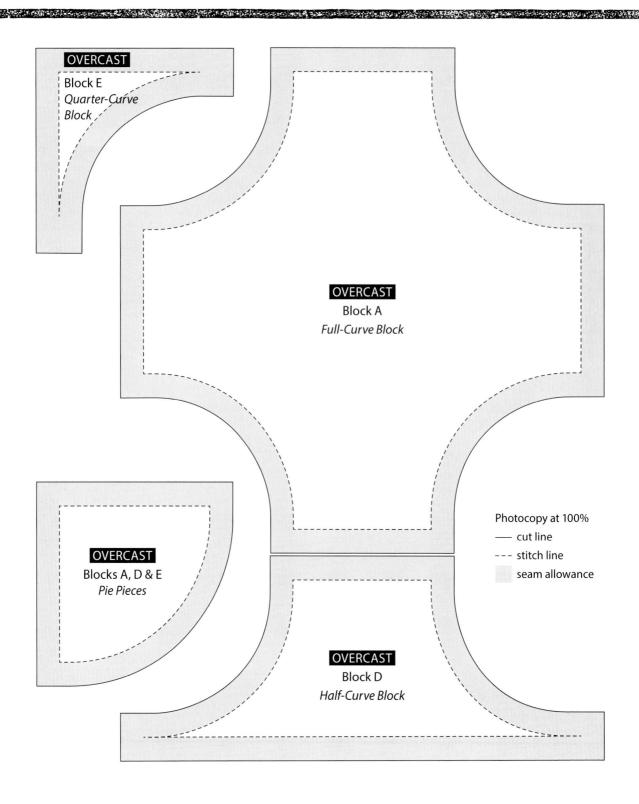

OVERCAST

Block E
Quarter-Curve Block

OVERCAST

Block A
Full-Curve Block

OVERCAST

Blocks A, D & E
Pie Pieces

OVERCAST

Block D
Half-Curve Block

Photocopy at 100%
— cut line
- - - stitch line
■ seam allowance

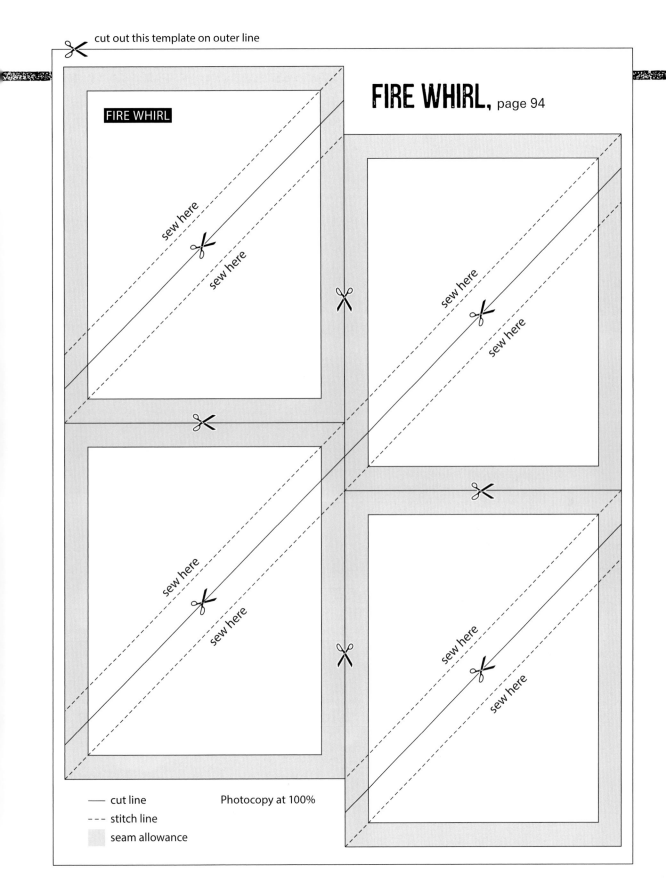

cut out this template on outer line

FIRE WHIRL, page 94

FIRE WHIRL

sew here

sew here

sew here

sew here

sew here

sew here

sew here

sew here

—— cut line

--- stitch line

seam allowance

Photocopy at 100%